T0129423

A Tale and Gateway to the Cosmic Laws and Produciaries
of Love and Light as Seen in the Great Elohim

AKASHIC ENLIGHTENMENT

AKASHIC RECORDS & BOOK OF TRUTH FOR DIVINE KNOWLEDGE, HEALING, & ASCENSION

Sherry Mosley, MSOM, CSP

BALBOA.
PRESS
A DIVISION OF HAY HOUSE

Balboa Press books may be ordered through booksellers or by contacting:

Balboa Press
A Division of Hay House
1663 Liberty Drive
Bloomington, IN 47403
www.balboapress.com
1 (877) 407-4847

Cover design by Sherry Mosley. Galaxy image from NASA galleries. All sketches by Sherry Mosley.

Print information available on the last page.

ISBN: 978-1-5043-9669-1 (sc)
ISBN: 978-1-5043-9769-8 (e)

Balboa Press rev. date: 05/24/2018

For all souls looking for this material.

Acknowledgments

A loving and sincere thank you for all of you amazing
souls as humans in this realm, you know who you are,
and those Divine Beings beyond, for all your help,
love and support in making this book possible.

We are all in this together.

Contents

Part Three: The Akashic Enlightenment Gateway Prayer

Part Four: Starting Your Akashic Enlightenment Experience

Foreword

How to Use This Book

This book is intended to be the story of how Akashic Enlightenment came to me, what it is and a simple guide on how you can now use it, showing you how to open and access your own Akashic Records/ Book of Life through the Book of Truth/Universal Truth/Laws of this Universe and beyond. The Akashic Enlightenment Gateway Prayer provided in this book was given to me March 28th, 2016 and I was asked to share it with the world. It is a gateway to the Cosmic Laws (Book of Truth) and the produciaries of Love and Light as seen in the Great Elohim, God/Source prior to Alpha and Omega or also known as the Creator God in the will of God/Source, that manifest Love and Light into form thus Akashic Enlightenment is a map to the mind that is one with God/Source/All That Is.

Parts of this book are directly scribed through Akashic Enlightenment, shamanic journey or from the Council of Light, and thus hold a divine resonance and transmission energy you may feel and at times it may not read cleanly but has been intact for vibrational divine transmission purposes.

For those of you that are A Course In Miracles students or teachers I have been told that ACIM is the key and Akashic Enlightenment is the door. Thus Akashic Enlightenment provides a practice of active access to the Book of Truth via your Akashic Records for in the moment personalized divine guidance and healing.

If you have any questions or wish to receive more instruction on how to access and use Akashic Enlightenment and your Akashic Records I do offer classes and consultations to take you deeper into your practice as well as personal Shamanic Akashic Record consults and healing.

I hope that you enjoy your experience and wish you peace, love and light and a wonderful journey.

Prologue

Denying the Call to Answering the Call

The very earliest inklings of my calling and abilities were when I was a little girl and would experience de ja vu quite frequently including seeing or premonitory dreaming things to come. Once I "saw" a small car accident my friend's mom was to have with me in the car and sure enough it happened. I also had a very real friendship with an invisible friend who I knew just too many details of for her to not exist on some plane, be it even unseen to the naked eye. I was also quite a sensitive child and would often get headaches with nausea, some to the point of vomiting, of which no one had an answer for back then, and a lot of allergies.

In high school amidst being drawn to dolphins and desiring to study dolphin intelligence, of which now I know is related to my Lemurian lifetimes and also a fascination with higher forms of being and communication, I started digging into books on the paranormal. In the mornings you could find me in the high school library digging through the Time Life book series *Mysteries of the Unknown*, full of stories and information on the paranormal and esoteric. Despite some of it freaking me out I couldn't stop reading them even at night before going to bed, and next to my mother's fascination with and thus my exposure to the the television series *The X-Files* at the time, this seemed to fit right in. The door was definitely opening.

During the summer between high school and college, the next quite accountable event was when my grandmother's life ended suddenly and her spirit visited me at my house. I didn't feel necessarily caught off guard and remember her telling me telepathically that she was fine where she was now which, while supposed to be comforting, only made her actual passing from this realm almost harder to accept. This was a new experience and close to home this time. Her spirit hung around their house for a while which I didn't share with my family and just allowed them their space to grieve and move on. I didn't feel comfortable to engage with her but was sure of her presence and even went to visit her in the World of the Dead in my shamanic training later in life where we did actually have a brief but meaningful conversation.

Then in 1998 while I was completing my bachelors degree at San Francisco State University two things revealing my healer and shamanic calling occurred. First, I enrolled in a minor in their Holistic Health program and absolutely fell in love with Chinese Medicine and the somewhat eccentric teacher we had teaching us, Angela Wu, who made it just all sound so absolutely magical and mystifying. I was so amazed with this class and Classical Chinese Medicine theory and their astrology based on the Five Elements that I almost went to her clinic to pursue it more, however, I just wasn't ready yet.

The second revealing experience to occur while a student at SFSU in 1998 was on the paranormal end of the spectrum. While I participated in their study abroad program taking me to Brunel University's design branch located in Egham Surrey England I lived in a dorm that was a converted mansion complete with gargoyles in the yard and which was of course, you guessed it, haunted. Upon my arrival I clearly sensed the presence of one if not more ghosts, beings, entities, deceased souls. They didn't seem particularly threatening but feeling their presence none the less was unwelcome. So, upon moving in I just said out loud that I had no interest in communicating with them and that this was to be my room for the duration of my stay and I'd like them to leave and leave me alone. And so they did. However, Europe is an old place and so visiting France during my time there brought more uncomfortable unwelcome encounters.

While staying at a pretty run down and old youth hostel in Paris I felt the presence of many deceased souls who were rather upset. Upon entering this place it just felt like a haunted house but being tired from traveling and in denial I didn't bother to find another place. Later that first night sleeping there I could see and feel numerous souls just circling around and around above the bed. I hated it and did what I could to ignore it jamming my headphones on and playing Enya as loud as I could while still trying to allow myself to fall asleep. It was no use. I clung to my boyfriend at the time, who was sound asleep. Come daylight I had maybe dozed off a few hours in the earlier morning and was now ready to get out of there. After a quiet morning of packing up and leaving to go to breakfast I asked my boyfriend if he'd felt the presence of anything when we were there. He was so relieved I said something claiming he hadn't wanted to say anything as to not freak me out but that that place totally freaked him out and he too had even felt other presences. We happily agreed to stay somewhere else and never went back. Unfortunately the videotape taken of this place was lost somewhere amidst moving.

Then in October of 2002, a year and a month after 9/11 had occurred, a wake up call to many I am sure, my calling began to present itself more clearly. I had just moved to Berkeley from San Francisco after having left my now flopped dot com job from the dot com bomb of 2001 and quitting my rather overnight successful straight edge electronic music disc jockey and producer career. There was no longer a need to stay in the city with left over skyrocketed rents and few jobs of interest. I was regrouping and taking time to reevaluate my life and life path. Of course, I unknowingly stumbled into a local bookstore that ended up introducing me to my shamanic lineage and healer calling, later revealing to be the roots of my strange paranormal encounters previously experienced in my life.

Lewin's Metaphysical Books on Ashby Avenue, now conveniently within walking distance of my new apartment was a magical place full of walls and tables stacked high with books on anything metaphysical and esoteric. I found myself visiting the bookshop rather frequently due to so much free time trying to figure out what it was I really wanted to do with my life. At the time I had no idea that this place was going to introduce me to and ignite my shamanic lineage roots and calling to be a healer.

I would hang out there regularly and grab what books I felt called to, something this place seemed created for, a vortex perhaps. It was here that I met a very sweet 80 something year old man who worked at the register a few days a week. He was very tall with a full beard with grey and white hair, kind eyes and a hug you'd remember forever. He was clearly a soul who it was not my first time meeting. We would chat on occasion at the counter when I'd go to pay for my books and one day he asked me if I was familiar with the Mayan Calendar. I shared with him that I was not and thus he decided to teach me.

The next time I returned to the bookstore he pulled out this bright yellow book with colorful artwork on the front cover and opened it up to show me these intricate shapes, Mayan glyphs I later found out, and very detailed charts that coincided with them. The book he used was the *Mayan Calendar Birthday Book* by Mary Fran Koppa along with some other photocopied pages from other knowledgeable texts on the subject. He explained how the symbols worked in the calendar and taught me how to do a basic Mayan Calendar birth chart. It was fun and I was intrigued with the accuracy of the descriptions of how it represented a person to be and what their path in this life was to be. Furthermore it described the energy and path a year was to take so as one could predict what future energies would be like. No wonder the Mayans had 2012 all mapped out!

I was grateful to learn this and experimented with friends and family who enjoyed having their birthdate chart done. It just came so naturally to me. I now realize this was based on my past Mayan lifetimes. I was already trained and experienced in such work which is part of my natural link to the Akashic Records now in this lifetime as the Mayans were already using the Akashic Records since early times.

Despite feeling excited with this work and doing good research on alternative health schools, trainings, credentials and certifications, I still couldn't decide or see how to move forward. I soon got distracted from my esoteric shamanic sprouting and alternative health research by allowing friends of my old life to pull me back into the music scene and a year later back to doing graphic design work that landed me in New York City! That is, until my Saturn's Return started pounding down my door in 2006. My destiny was not to be so easily denied.

It was August of 2006 and I was living in a gross apartment, compared to my California standards, in of course Hell's Kitchen of New York City. It was here that I ironically had the height of my

Saturn's Return. Being a Sun and Moon in Capricorn and Saturn being Capricorn's ruling planet it was quite intense and pulled to the surface my calling I'd been resisting following and committing to.

At that time I randomly bought five books on Amazon about Shamanism and I knew I had a calling to help others. Previously back in 2002 during my research I had considered many alternative health schools like naturopathic medicine school, massage school and holistic health and was finally enrolled in a basic holistic health online class with Clayton College, for those of you who remember that somewhat illegitimate online institution. Come fall that year I had decided that if I was going to really do this life change to follow my calling I first needed to get back to my roots on the West Coast.

So in October of 2006 I moved back to San Francisco, although Portland was close in the running for their amazing Naturopathic school I'd had my eye on. NCNM, National College of Naturopathic Medicine now called Natural University of Naturopathic Medicine. I felt I just needed to come back to my roots in San Francisco.

So once resettled into San Francisco again and working at Netflix as a User Interface Designer and Art Director, such a fun, amazing and well paying job, I started having some health issues. I knew something was off and despite the money and fun with such a great company I felt empty inside and realized I had once again paused on perusing my calling and the wounded shaman was birthing due to this.

So in 2007 I found a naturopath who started treating me but who finally suggested I go get acupuncture. I went to a five element acupuncturist and wow! I loved it and started feeling better right away and knew I had to pursue this. So that summer I planned a trip to Portland to finally visit NCNM to check out their naturopathic program I'd originally felt drawn to and once there felt totally drawn to natural medicine and their Classical Chinese Medicine program. I returned home elated knowing I was finally going in the right direction.

That same year I also saw a psychic a co-worker at Netflix had suggested. I saw her twice. Once before my visit to NCNM in Portland and once after. She told me I was psychic and encouraged me to get some sort of psychic training and also said due to my blood line that I'd do best with the shamanic route and if I felt drawn to Chinese Medicine to pursue that as well.

So I started researching shamanism online and found a local practitioner who also practiced reiki. I called her and said, "I think I am a shaman and don't know where to start". In doing some sessions with her my abilities and calling were quickly revealed. This was clearly not my first lifetime doing this work. I was seeing what she was seeing and tapping into what she was doing and more, to the point that she asked me, how are you doing that. Of course I had no answer to that question as I was wondering that myself! All I knew was that it was clearly calling me.

So I did some reiki and shamanism training with her and this was my introduction to shamanism. I learned about power animals and shamanic journeying along with the reiki training I received. It was an intense experience partially cracking my third eye open at one point where I fell to the floor with so much energy and information coming in at once. It was a process to learn how to do this in a way that worked with my physical body that my soul was so eager to throw into the deep end now that the doors were open and it could finally soar freely.

At this time I also enrolled into an introductory Chinese Medicine class at ACTCM in San Francisco. After feeling so excited about that I then enrolled in a weekend Five Element training at Acupuncture and Integrative Medicine College in Berkeley which I also loved and felt so drawn to that I knew it was time to commit.

So, January of 2008 I left Netflix due to health issues that according to them seemed to be calling for a required period of disability leave and enrolled at Acupuncture and Integrative Medicine College in Berkeley and began my calling, never to look back.

While in school I overheard someone talking about their shamanic friend who was also an author and who wrote a book on shamanism and was having a book signing in San Francisco that weekend. I went. I loved it. I asked him about him and his wife's shamanic retreats down in South America. Feeling intimidated to go on such a trip while my health was still recovering a bit his wife, also a shamanic practitioner and psychotherapist, suggested I check out the Foundation for Shamanic Studies as their program was as close to what I'd experience in a retreat in South America. After some research I went to see a shamanic practitioner in the East Bay who had trained with the Foundation and received shamanic healing and further guidance and confirmation for my path. I was feeling good and confident with it all.

In 2009 while still attending Acupuncture & Integrative Medicine College, I started my training with the Foundation for Shamanic Studies. I took some introductory shamanism courses learning basic divination journeying and how to retrieve power animals. It was so natural and I greatly enjoyed it. So in 2010 I took more intensive shamanic training and became a Certified Shamanic Practitioner (CSP) and Shamanic Journey Counselor. I took to it all quickly and it felt very natural to me as well as gave me a container to put my already existing psychic abilities into. My psychic and empathic abilities had previously had me more or less at their mercy for the greater part of my life up until then by me unintentionally taking on others energy which is what had led to some of the health problems I'd been having, as well as at times telling people things they were clearly not aware of consciously and my least favorite, as you already know, being contacted by upset or confused deceased souls. That last one use to paralyze me in fear until I got this proper shamanic training on how to use my abilities properly. Once trained it was time to practice.

I practiced my own journeying, healing and divination work with friends, with some clients and by joining a local drum circle while continuing my Asian medicine studies which took the majority of my energy and gave me less time to practice.

In 2014 while in my last year of Asian medicine school I was introduced to the book *A Course In Miracles* of which I did the guided lessons of and later worked on reading the text. For those not familiar with *A Course In Miracles*, it is a scribed text and lessons from Jesus aligning one with Christ Consciousness and Universal Knowledge through its reading and proper assimilation and application of. I feel that reading it and doing the lessons brought my awareness to a higher level, a key if you will, that further revealed and unlocked the doors to higher realms in my shamanic practice which I was to later find out was exactly true.

Finally in 2015 after completing my Masters of Science in Oriental Medicine, as my guides had instructed me to do, and more fully dedicating to my private practice, I dove deep into shamanic journeying. There were some upsetting events that occurred at that time and our planet's energy was shifting more and more which all drove me to journey regularly for clarity. A year of daily journeying to be specific. However, amidst getting clarity on events and guidance, the journey my spirit guides, teachers and Angels took me on was not expected though clearly all planned out in my soul's higher plan and leading to Akashic Enlightenment.

PART ONE

The Awakening

CHAPTER 1

Angel Channeling, Shamanic Journeying, Light Beings, the Book of Life/Akashic Records

Angel Channeling

May of 2015 was a huge month of transformation for me. Aside from my regular shamanic journeying practice, I started doing my own Angel channeling upon suggestion in a session with a shamanic drum circle peer of mine who I saw on May 7th. Although that instruction had been to do my own channeling with my great great grandmother, who was a very powerful medicine woman in her time of which I was a lineage of, it took a direction of its own, or maybe I should say SHE took it in another direction than maybe I'd expected or had no idea would have occurred.

So, I did a little online research and put together my own channeling ritual using an angel meditation mp3, some relaxing alpha brainwave sounds in the background, a prayer for protection I found online, and an original version of the Lords Prayer which is known to hold channeling capabilities. I also gathered some powerful crystals including moldavite, angelite, angel aura quartz, and amethyst.

When I did this first channeling as automatic writing I was rather surprised by not only my great great grandmother showing up in the room but nameless Beings of Light followed by Archangel Metatron who then introduced Ascended Master Jesus who showed up. I realize now I shouldn't have been surprised considering the ritual I put together and clearly what my great great grandmother had in store for me, but here it was all the same.

So I started doing this channel writing regularly this way and soon Middle World Journeying (shamanic journey in this realm, not to the Upper or Lower World, but in the spirit world or world beyond the veil of this 3rd dimension) with Archangel Metatron, Archangel Michael, the Seraphim and Ascended Master Jesus. In these sessions I received many various very powerful messages about my mission, being a child of God and needing to tend to my flock, and past life information from Atlantis.

Angel Hierarchy/Choirs of Angels:
Seraphim
Cherabim
Thrones
Dinamie/Dominions
Virtues
Powers/Potentates/Dynamis
Principles
Archangels
Angels

Light Beings & Shamanic Journeying to the Akashic Records/Book of Life

At this same time I was doing this channel work I also kept doing my frequent practice of traditional shamanic journeying via listening to drumming sounds. Soon enough the Being of Light that had shown up in the Angel channeling session now showed up in my shamanic journeys.

My spirit teacher Teki in these shamanic journeys taught me to merge with the Being of Light in the shamanic journey telling me that this was actually my true state.

Background on Light Beings

Jesus is often referred to as 'Christ' which is actually a reference to KRYST which are the letters of the first sounds of all creation, KA RA YA SA TA AA LA. Thus Christ/KRYST is the energy the man Jesus learned, or was incarnated on Earth to align with in the ancient mystery schools of his time on Earth and thus did so to show everyone how to do it. Thus, he became called 'Christ' though Christ Consciousness is actually KRYST(AL) or Original Creation Consciousness of being a Krystal/Crystal/Diamond Body/ Christos Blueprint/Light Being and many other beings have done this and have also become Ascended Masters now part of the Council of Light as Christ/Jesus has.

This explains why my spirit guide Teki had me merging with a Being of Light telling me it was my original state. He meant it was my state as aligned with the inception of all creation which my soul naturally connects to being a part of Source/God/Creation.

After practicing doing this a few times in the shamanic journeys, I merged with the Being of Light in one journey and my spirit teacher Teki introduced me to the Akashic Records. The Records here were represented by these large opaque plates that I would ascend through like a membrane and feel a very dense vibrational shift in the shamanic journey. It was very clear I was crossing over into another realm, a higher vibration, in the journey. In this introduction to the Akashic Records he showed to me the universe above pointing to all of the stars saying I was composed of star dust. He then instructed me to study the Akashic Records further.

May 16, 2015 - Shamanic Journey to the Upper World: Introduction to the Akashic Records/Book of Life

I play the shamanic journey drumming and put on the headphones, place my eye cover on over my moldavite and white azeztutlie placed on my forehead, state my intention and go up to the Upper World to meet my spirit teacher.

Spirit Teacher Teki sweeps me up and takes me up and we sit on the grass. He has me laugh out loud at all the beauty.

Spirit Teacher Teki: This is all in your heart and right now, shining out from your heart.

Now pointing to all the stars in the sky and putting them into the foundation. The stars are forever and eternity they are the many lives you share. That's what's being collected right now. You're collecting this information.

I get the sense this is something about the Akashic Records.

Spirit Teacher Teki: Come on we're going to go forward in time.

I see images from my future.

Spirit Teacher Teki: This is your future (as he's showing me these glowing energetic plates). Your reality your world is based on is unhinging. It feels uncomfortable but you are just moving to a higher level where things will flow much easier. This is necessary.

I see these plates unlocking and breaking apart and I float up above them. I feel a higher vibration in my body. There is an ease and flow to things now. I don't have to try to do things any more.

Spirit Teacher Teki: Yes, exactly. Everything will just be. There won't be the suffering like you've experienced. Just let these changes happen. You can go and read up on the Akashic Records. I'm showing you your Akashic Records because you have to know it exists. You have to break these plates. (The plates that were the between the world and the Akashic Records.)

Me: How do I do that?

Spirit Teacher Teki: You're already doing it. The crystals, the mediations and the channeling. Don't listen to your egos mind saying you're wasting your time. All these things are necessary for your growth. To bring this future to you. I'm showing you now the Akashic Records. Just keep doing your spiritual work. Your intuitive work, look up Akashic. Keep going keep following. Keep reading your intuitive book (a book on intuition I was reading at the time). This is enough for you now.

Me: Thank you.

Spirit Teacher Teki: Very welcome. Peace be with you.

So I began this research and after a few more times of crossing through the plates in the shamanic journeys to the Akashic Records, Ascended Master Jesus showed up in the journey now as my Akashic Record and Beyond spirit teacher. He began teaching me and showing me how to absolve or forgive my karma in the Records, furthermore saying I am to teach and heal people with the Akashic Records and that he enabled me to change other's Records in order to give them karmic healing and healing of anything that's going on. He shared that I've already been doing this on a certain level and that I just wasn't really aware of what was going on and not in control of it and now I am.

I'll admit after this I was a bit freaked out or overwhelmed with what was happening so I called up one of my shamanic peers. I explained what was happening with the Angel channeling and the shamanic journeys saying that I just no longer felt human. He then said, "oh so an Angel then". I hadn't realized how that affected me at the time but it sunk in. Later I found out that yes indeed I am what is called an Earth Angel and part of the 144,000 Angels here to help humanity shift. My friend also suggested I do a journey to the Thrones Angels which I had to look up as I'd never heard of them. I found out that they are the third rank of Angels who also happen to work with the Seraphim, so it would make sense to make a visit to them after my Angel channeling and automatic writing work with them earlier. I also found out that the Thrones meet with God/Source directly to find out how to help people and the universe and how the other Angels can best do these missions God/Source assigns to them or are God's Will being acted out. This makes them very wise. They also explain God's/Source's Will to people who are asking or praying for guidance. Perfect!

May 18ᵗʰ 2015 - Shamanic Journey to the Upper World: Thrones Angels to Experience and Learn Healing

I do my usual shamanic journey ritual listening to the drums with eyes covered and go up to the Upper World.

My spirit teacher Teki is here and says this is your journey. He walks me up to the Akashic Records after I merge with the Being of Light of who I've been told is my natural state. I'm thrown into one of the Records of the Akashic Records.

Spirit Teacher Teki: You've done all this before. Don't you remember? In your sleep...you've done this already. We just wanted you to know you've done this already.

The Thrones Angels are there and want to take me above the Akashic Records. We are outside the Records up in outer space. It's all black with stars.

Thrones Angels: This is what it all is. We have to teach you.

There are all these glowing Beings of Light and I feel nervous. They want me to go through this doorway that's glowing white.

Thrones Angels: (Pointing to the stars) This is where it all starts. There are stars and they are arranged into patterns and their dust. This dust is formed into plates that then form the Akashic Records. And then they slide them down into their rows (timelines). Now, your question is "what do you want me to do with the Akashic Records in healing people?" We want you to take them to their Records, teach them to journey to the Upper World, meet their teacher and go into their Records and rearrange the dust.

Me: What does this do?

Thrones Angels: It allows people to live the life to exactly what they want, not what is karmicly written any more. You get to actually choose exactly what you want. There is no predestination, there is no path, there is no soul purpose. You choose once you're already here, everything will be wiped clean, you'll be reset and you get to consciously choose what you want. This is a big shift.

I see Ascended Master Jesus come down from out of or near the white glowing doorway. Teki seems afraid like this might be too much for me. And the Thrones say that's why Jesus is here, he'll protect you.

Me: I feel scared.

Spirit Teacher Teki: If Jesus is with you you'll be safe.

There is the white door that is open. I go in with Jesus.

Ascended Master Jesus: This is God.

It's nothing but white empty space like in the movie the Matrix.

Me: What do you want me to do with the Akashic Records? Why are you showing me all of this?

Ascended Master Jesus: Quiet.

A yellow ball of light appears in front of us floating towards us and he puts it in the center of my chest. I have trouble talking (long sigh) as energy shifts.

Ascended Master Jesus: Wonderful, perfect fit, you're perfect for this job. You're no longer who you used to be. It'll take those around you a while to get used to this but the energy they feel coming off of you will be so strong that it'll be ok with them. It'll feel ok it won't feel logical but they'll know it's ok.

Jesus strokes my head. We walk back out of the glowing door and the Thrones Angels are there. That's it. Then we go down to the Akashic Records and the Thrones start wiping away all the shelves or rows in front of me wiping wiping wiping them all away.

Thrones Angels: What do you want?

Me: I feel really nervous anxious and scared right now. I don't know if I should be doing this. Can you help me?

The Thrones help me fill in something that's in my highest good. There is a blur of images representing a happy life and joy, healing of past traumas. Things have been shifted and the Records are now glowing gold.

Thrones Angels: This is how to live the life of an Ascended Master.

And that was my introduction to doing healing work in the Akashic Records in a shamanic journey.

CHAPTER 2

Shamanic Journeys Bring the Rainbow Body / Light Body / Ascension / Enlightenment and This Book

As instructed I continued studying the Akashic Records more with what I found through fellow shamanic peers, teachers, books on the subject and continued journeying. Amidst this venture my spirit teacher Ascended Master Jesus took me on a series of shamanic journeys to the world of the deceased or passed on souls over the rainbow, to the Tree of Life, Source/God/Creator, to see multiple dimensions or timelines and how they work, the Lemurian Palace, Atlantis Palace, 7th Heaven, my home soul planet, and more. Amongst these visits were teachings, initiations and energy alignments, transmissions and attunements that would fill their own book and the first instructions to write a book.

I really had no idea what journey I was really embarking on when I did these shamanic journeys and Akashic Record work and just went the way I was shown, surrendered. In retrospect what took place was what I believe was my soul awakening, my Ascension, my aligning with my Light Body, crossing over the rainbow bridge (Rainbow Body), touching Enlightenment and coming back with the instructions now to teach it, as the Thrones Angels had earlier informed me was my "mission".

Following are the series of shamanic journeys and Akashic Record work in which some quite astounding rituals and rites of passage took place preparing me for this mission of this book you are reading right now. I will share a few of what I consider to be pinnacle moments.

June 5th, 2015 - Shamanic Journey to the Upper World: Rainbow Chakra Attunement to Healed Light Being

I go up to the Upper World to meet my spirit teacher and up to the Akashic Records.

Spirit Teacher Jesus: Your Records are blessed. What you want is what will be.

Me: What do you mean?

Spirit Teacher Jesus: Aligning your energy with that which what you want.

Me: How?

Spirit Teacher Jesus: Your heart.

Jesus asks the Masters, Teachers, Loved Ones, Beings of Light to heal my heart for what I want to be to be in that energy. They put white light in my heart. Jesus takes me up to a white door.

Spirit Teacher Jesus: She wants healing so what she wants can be manifested.

Light comes from behind and goes up and down my spine and body in a rainbow going through my body to the front. Now golden light comes on through the crown of my head and goes all way down as my chakras begin to light up from the bottom all the way up. I see all the colors. And I see 2 or 3 chakras above my head light up.

Spirit Teacher Jesus: You're a healed Light Being. Your spirit will allow you to have what you want. We know that your body suffers certain things but when it suffers just remember to ask what it really wants.

Me: I feel good. It looks so pretty.

Spirit Teacher Jesus: Your Records are blessed and you've been attuned. Eat food and rest today and let this take place in your body. Don't overwork today. Drink plenty of water.

Me: Ok

July 19th, 2015 - Shamanic Journey to the Upper World: Rainbow Lighbody Adventure

I play the shamanic journey drumming and put on the headphones, place my eye cover on over my moldavite and white azeztutlie placed on my forehead, state my intention and go up to the Upper World to meet my spirit teacher.

Teki greats me and has me again merge with the light being that descends to the grassy hill we are standing on. A Buddha type female face God with all the arms on her shows up (I had to look this up after the journey as I had no previous knowledge of these beings. It was Shiva.) She's smiling at me saying you're with us now. She's laughing joyfully. She says she thinks it's funny saying "you're one of us now and you don't even know it and that's what makes it so great. It's true humbleness you don't even know".

Teki takes me up through the plates up to the Akashic Records to a guide of the Records.

Me: Who's this white glowing being?

Glowing Guide Being of the Akashic Records: Just be here now. We know that's hard because you see the faults in the past but they don't hold true now. Do you understand? Focusing there brings them here and you want to focus on what we're showing you to bring that here.

Me: I see. Can you show me again what I need to focus on to bring it here?

And Jesus comes down. Reminds me of the karmic free life I've chosen. If you choose the past then you'll live a life in the past. If you choose a life that you're manifesting then you'll live that.

Jesus is telling them to show me the Records that show the manifestations of what I want...what is the highest order. A slide show of images of an idyllic life flash by like movie screens floating in the air each playing their own movie like the moving paintings in Harry Potter or the transparent screens seen in movies.

Me: Why does this one image feel so much thicker or heavier like I'm really in it?

I see the image from all different angles, like I'm actually there. My feeling is that this is what's happening in another dimension.

Spirit Teacher Jesus: It's a little different than the Akashic Records. It's happening in another dimension and its being brought into the Records to be shown to you.

Me: I'm not really sure how that works.

Spirit Teacher Jesus: Come back later and we'll explain it but not today. Just know that the image is what you need to focus on now.

Me: Ok

Jesus is calling me up so I go up to him on a plane up above the Akashic Records. He takes me through this white door to a room that is all white like that scene in the Matrix. Everything is white light and he says to have a healing done on me, to align everything for today. A golden ball of light comes and scans my body up and down in front. Then through my body back and forth back and forth, like scrubbing the inside of my body. Then each of the chakras start lighting up one by one from the bottom up. Red, orange, yellow...very important chakra, green, blue, violet, magenta, 3 white light ones above the head. Then they pull what looks like a white glowing string from the top. It feels like a tug in my body and pulls up on the energy of them all. A beam from the top of my head shoots up and at an arc, a rainbow arc appears. Jesus says to follow the rainbow arc. We go and follow the rainbow arc up literally traveling along a rainbow to the end of the rainbow. I don't know where we are. I feel a little scared.

I call to Spirit Teacher Teki. He comes and reassures I'm ok as I'm with Jesus.

So we are in this other place and there are all these other souls here. They look dark, like black ghost type images with no face. Jesus explains they look dark but they aren't bad and these are ascended souls. They've died and come here. This is where you'll come this time. And he takes me through all the beings. He explains they look dark to me now because I'm not really here I'm just visiting and that when I'm actually here it'll be in color and light. He explains he just doesn't want me to get overwhelmed and distracted because he wants to show me something.

He takes me to this tree. It's huge and green with dark thick bark and grass all around it and blue skies here that fade into the dark black around where all the souls are hanging out.

Spirit Teacher Jesus: This is the tree of life. Eat the fruit from this tree.

I eat the fruit. It's falling on me from the tree. I'm eating it as fast as I can. He says yes eat as much as you can till you're full. And now I'm just taking in these orange globes, they look like oranges, off of the tree. And I'm full up to my neck. It all pops inside of my body and it releases a juice inside my body and in my head to the crown of my head it pushes up. Up above it shoots a golden light above my head forming another arc.

Jesus says let's go on this arc. And we go.

Spirit Teacher Jesus: This is the space time continuum arc and this is how you get to other dimensions. I just wanted to show you now where the image came from.

And I just see all these lines of rows. They are just endless rows. And it's all these parallel lives like strings. Golden strings. And I see images hanging off of each one like a movie film.

Spirit Teacher Jesus: When you're in the Records you can pull images from any of these lives, parallel dimensional lives and bring them into this one and it's stronger and easier when you're having a karmic free life because they already exist in another dimension and you're usually picking up on them and that's why you choose that when you're living a karmic free life.

Me: Ok.

So he's explaining living a karmic free life is not just living in grace. I feel amazingly ok with all of this.

Spirit Teacher Jesus: It's because you're already aligned with all of it.

So I just see all the strings hanging there. We're standing on this glowing golden path. Jesus is next to me.

Spirit Teacher Jesus: So you can use this to create the life that you want when you don't know what to put in your Records. You can ask the Record keepers or me for a suggestion from one of these parallel dimensions. That way you're taking an option not based on karma but is based on manifestation of your soul but from another place that is karmic free.

Spirit Teacher Jesus: Understand?

Me: Yes. A little overwhelmed....wow. It's pretty cool. I don't have words.

Spirit Teacher Jesus: (He laughs) Wow is perfect.

He's showing all the strings go up in the air to God/Creation/Source. It's a giant white glowing ball of light with the strings coming down from there into these strings in the many dimensional lives.

Spirit Teacher Jesus: Your soul light is part of THAT light.

Me: Oooooooh. I have a feeling it'll be helpful to draw this when I got back.

Spirit Teacher Jesus: So when you die your soul goes back to THIS piece, ultimately. And then it chooses all these different dimensions. So your soul, because it's part of this light fragments into all these other dimensions.

Me: Ok

Spirit Teacher Jesus: It is the piece in this light that is most like the piece that you are. It's not so much an identity as it is a piece of sand.

Spirit Teacher Jesus: So in this life another person is the piece of sand that is paradimensional to yours.

Me: Ok. What does that mean then?

Spirit Teacher Jesus: They too have ultimate power to have a karmic free life if they choose that but most are not choosing that and this is where things are getting divided. We are trying to help them wake up. They will. You just have to keep doing what we're telling you.

Me: So what happens when there are two pieces in one dimension?

Spirit Teacher Jesus: The chunk of the what you call the soul is then bigger in this dimension than it is in the other dimensions so you make one chunk that was split so when it joins together it kinda becomes the ultimate dimension because there's more of that soul chunk from Source in one dimension. It then becomes the highest dimension of all the dimensions. But you have to do the work to join these parts. That's why it's very uncommon. That's why even in all these other strands they are not even choosing their karmic free life because you've met this other part of you it's now triggered this other sequence of events.

Me: Ok

Spirit Teacher Jesus: Let's go back down.

We go back to the tree with fruit, follow rainbow light back over.

Me: I don't like leaving. I like it there.

Spirit Teacher Jesus: I know. It's your ultimate Home which you can visit.

Me: Ok. Omg I'm just so happy and high from all of this.

I'm in the white area and I can't stop laughing I'm just so happy.

Spirit Teacher Jesus: This is your soul at peace because it knows.

Me: Ok. Huh. I keep seeing an image and to draw it. This is an important image to document isn't it.

Spirit Teacher Jesus: Yes you can try to find an artist to document it for you.

I'm coming down from the high a little bit.

Spirit Teacher Jesus: You can come back whenever you want.

Me: Ok

We go. I go down to the Records.

Me: Ah man I really liked it there.

Spirit Teacher Jesus: Now that you've been there and touched there there is a line of energy that you will carry with you.

We go back down to Teki. And the Asian faced god is there. The god with an Asian face with all the arms, looks like a combo of Buddha and Ganesha. She just sits there laughing in the sky of the upper world. She's clapping all of her hands giggling saying "this is so great...you don't even know who you are yet".

Teki: You can talk to her more later she'll be there.

Me: What did I do that all of this happened?

Spirit Teacher Jesus: You're ready

Me: Ok

Call back drums.

I have come to realize those journeys were my strongest "awakening". I remember feeling like a different person afterwards, SO high and SO blissful. I felt like I had left all that I thought had mattered behind me. I'm still trying to find why it happened exactly and am just told that it was my studies, shamanic journey practice, and because it was just my time. I realize now I was truly being shown the basics of living a karmic free life, a life free of living in past thoughts, conditions, patterns, and beliefs. I also see now that that is what so many others now term "manifestation", or "cocreating", or being the God/Source you are and creating it all through first seeing the image of it, what I was doing in my shamanic journeys, thus allowing that feeling of seeing that image sink in and then that allows it to manifest in this reality once our mind has aligned with this image the Higher Self has provided, in this case from a parallel dimension, a reality outside of everything holding it back from being. Amazing. And this is exactly what connecting to our Higher Self is for. Receiving this divine guidance outside of the control of the ego mind and it's doubts and fear to move into love and creation and allow our soul to live at it's highest level and ability as God/Source has intended.

Since then I have also discovered some very confirming knowledge about the Tibetan Rainbow Body and the many stories and image depictions of Jesus seen with a light body and an aura of or sitting on a rainbow relating to Ascension. Traditionally aligning with the Rainbow Body is seen when one transcends all suffering and attains a state of complete union with the universe and the consciousness of creation. It is commonly termed Ascension or Enlightenment meaning transforming out of separate selfishness, negative ego, into service of Universal or Divine Will. This very much sounds like all the lessons I was given during this period of time and the mission I was sent on.

I also have to admit the Academy Award nominated song the *Rainbow Connection* performed by Kermit the Frog (Jim Henson) in Jim Henson's *The Muppet Movie* and *The Muppet Show* in the 1980s used to deeply strike me with an almost eery feeling I couldn't understand as a child but I knew it meant something deep and important. Now when I listen to it, I can't help but feel tears well up as now I know what it was really talking about and what I was feeling or remembering even then…"have you been half asleep, and have you heard voices, I've heard them calling my name…It's something that I'm supposed to be". That says it all. There are no accidents.

After this I continued my studies practicing in the Akashic Records more and come September that year I learned this was not a new modality to my soul. At one point I received this in the Akashic Records:

September, 2015 - Me Reading My Akashic Records

You're from Atlantis. You're from Egypt. You're from the Mayans. You were part of all these ancient civilizations. You have many past lives there. You were a great healer. Like a sorcerer. Something with my hands. Using my hands for healing. And I feel my hands throbbing right now. Glowing. Healing touch. You're a conduit.

You're waking up to these truths now. I see pyramids and Atlantis. And I was a Light Being in all these lives. My hands are just throbbing. Why are my hands throbbing? This is who you are. You've always been a healer of the hands.

This is the last lifetime. You're ascending after this one. This is why you're waking up to all the other lives before. You're returning Home. I see a glowing Angel being. You'll return Home back to the Light. You've come here to do this work. To help other people wake up to the Light that they can go back Home to. When your work here is complete you can go back Home. We're sorry you've forgotten for so many lifetimes but it's ok.

It is quite clear to me now that this was all definitely my soul waking me up to who I'd forgotten I already am and why I am here.

The Inception of This Book

Following these journeys were more initiations and teachings on my soul and where I'm from. Among these came the following journey that I was to write this book you're now reading.

December, 2015 - Shamanic Journey to Upper World introduces writing this book.

I am with my spirit teacher Ascended Master Jesus, in the Upper World, through and beyond the Akashic Records in higher realms. I see this golden body within mine or go into mine. This is my golden body. I am now standing in golden light with him (Ascended Master Jesus).

Spirit Teacher Jesus: There is no separating this. Go ahead and try, see what happens. You can't break this, it'll just cause suffering. Sorry this is so hard for you. This has all been built this way for a reason. You built this this way. You came here to do this. You're ready to see what you came here to do. It's time.

Now we're walking further into the white space this time. There was a jungle we walked through and now into a cave. And we come to a pedestal with a crystal on it.

Me: This is what they showed me in that Angel channeling.

Spirit Teacher Jesus: Yes, these are all the same. We are all the same. These are all the same places for you. We are all working together to help you with this.

I approach the pedestal with the golden crystal on it.

Me: What is that?

Spirit Teacher Jesus: Golden Crystal Key to Ultimate Love. Once you take this there is no going back.

He takes it and he hands it to me. I hold it and I drop it as I feel energy go through my body. He picks it up and I hold it again. It's a golden shard crystal about 10 inches long. It melts into my hands and goes up my arms and it covers my body in golden melted light, like liquid gold covering my body and I'm glowing gold.

Me: Ok now what?

Spirit Teacher Jesus: That was it. That wasn't so bad was it?

Me: No.

He leads me out and we come back to the white space.

Me: Ok, so that's what I came here for?

Spirit Teacher Jesus: Yes, to manifest Golden Light and Love.

Me: I like that.

Then I'm in a library or old looking building with stone walls and everything seems lit by candle light. He shows me a golden calligraphy pen writing in this huge book, like a scene out of Harry Potter (or as referenced to in the book *The Lost Book of Enki*). As I write the text is glowing golden light.

Spirit Teacher Jesus: Like the *A Course In Miracles* you're going to write a book.

Me: A blog?

Spirit Teacher Jesus: No, a book.

Me: (Sigh) Oh boy.

Spirit Teacher Jesus: *Advances in Journeying and the Technology of the Light in Love: How to Open the Doors of the Crystal Palace of the Beyond.*

(He's referring to this book you are reading now as I'm told later in another journey "the title does not matter, it is where you go and where you lead them, the energy is the same" and that is where this book takes you.)

Me: The crystal palace of the beyond?

Spirit Teacher Jesus: Yes you've already been there, the crystal palace in the 7th Heaven. It's the gateway to your soul.

Me: Right, ok.

Spirit Teacher Jesus: You are now going to start downloading chapters of this book.

Me: Oh shit, seriously?

Spirit Teacher Jesus: Yes.

Me: Geez. People are going to think I'm nuts.

Spirit Teacher Jesus: People are looking for confirmation of what you're going to write.

Me: Oh, ok.

Spirit Teacher Jesus: Go to your Records and ask for the downloads of this book. Go there and download. They will tell you. Don't worry. First you have to write the book. By the time it's ready to come out you'll be ready. Just write it now just like you're writing everything right now.

Me: Ok.

Spirit Teacher Jesus: Go now you're done.

After this I kept doing shamanic journeying, receiving more lessons and alignments, and Akashic Record work, but felt unsure on if any book material was really coming. Now that I'm sitting here writing this sharing everything I wrote down over the last few years I see what he meant by "just write it now like you're writing everything right now". It all just came to me in bits and pieces.

PART TWO

Akashic Enlightenment: Akashic Records & Book of Truth

CHAPTER 3

What is the Book of Life (Akashic Records) And How Does It Work

The Book of Life, also known as the Akashic Records, is an ancient energetic book, record or database of every thought, emotion, feeling, word and action ever to exist, is existing or will exist. Imagine it as the consciousness cloud or like an energetic Internet to which you naturally have a connection to via your soul and it's own expansive record, and you just need a browser or device to access it. This is where having an Akashic Record gateway prayer, like the one you are being taught here, comes in and why technicians, like myself, are given gateway prayers and easy access to them. So we can teach others how to use them at this time for their own soul evolution, Ascension and self enlightenment.

Doing your soul's growth work through accessing the Akashic Records allows you to step out of those repeating patterns, more associated with 3rd density awareness, and to become more conscious or aware by being aligned with who you are at your soul level, clear karma, understand soul contracts, the positives and negatives of situations and why they are happening and over all what your soul's plan is. Overall it will also bring you to a higher vibration and awareness as humanity is transitioning to in these great times of change.

In this awareness you can prevent being in repeat over and over again in this lifetime and extending over into other lives until you get it and can finally just move onto getting what your soul is really trying to tell you. The reason that you are really here. Then you can rise above the current matrix system that keeps you in that repeating unconscious reincarnation loop. In this greater awareness and connection to higher self, your soul and thus to Source, you can then begin to see what can be gained from certain situations instead of getting caught up in the ego's game of avoiding what is really going on and distracting one with other tasks, thoughts and behaviors. Such behavior can get to the point of causing disharmony in one's health and well being and ultimately leading to many common illnesses, or dis-ease, as it takes you the long way around on your soul's path back to Source, a process referred to as Ascension or Self Enlightenment. What is meant here is that you came here for a reason. Your soul has a plan and it is in your Akashic Record. In the past only very select few had access to such Divine Knowledge, but now as our planet becomes more conscious due it's own evolutionary process, we too are becoming more aware of who we really are.

This Ascended state is an original state for humans of which we have forgotten about and have been separated from for many reasons and at which time we are all waking up to again as we remember this once Divine connection we all used to have.

Diagram of How the Akashic Records Work

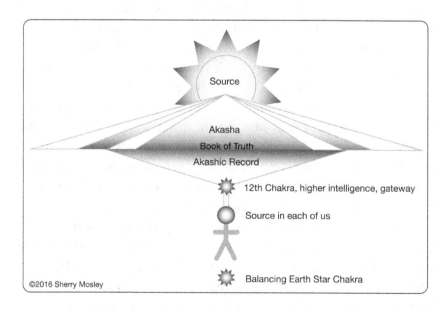

Source is in each of us via our soul, yet without connection to Source we often forget who we really are. The Akasha is the in-between, between us and our soul and connected to our Akashic Records of the greater Akasha to Source. The Akashic Records are the translator and communicator making sure we remember our connection and it provides the road map back home to Source.

Our 12th chakra, or Soul Star chakra located 6 to 12 inches from the top of the head, has been shut down for a long time and is now awakening again due to planetary shifts and the Universe waking up over all. Just as a rainy day affects us, so do the planets and Universal changes that are occurring now. These occurrences can all be seen as originally tracked by the Mayans with their calendars and buildings encoding time and measuring human consciousness as they had access to the Akashic Records to do so.

Finally, the Balancing Earth Star Chakra, located 6 to 12 inches below our feet, is the balancing version of our higher consciousness grounding it here to Earth, of which we are conduits for. Thus we bring this consciousness down through us to Earth which is also an important role we play in this. We are grounding rods, but need to clear up our reception as it has been lost, forgotten or the signal has been clouded with heavier energies.

Akashic Records, Time and Awakening

In the Akashic Records all time is at the same time, meaning past, present and future are all now. Thus, accessing the past affects the present and future simultaneously. Accessing the past can range from receiving knowledge from this life to lifetimes including Egypt, Atlantis, Lemuria, the Angelic realm, other planets, ancient Mayan civilizations or as a soul who was a soul part of famous healers and teachers like Jesus or Buddha and more.

The point here is to gain knowledge of who you really are at a soul level, from any point in time, learn from or gain knowledge from past mistakes and learnings and why what is happening now in relation to it in order to clear it from repeating or be inspired by it and motivated forward on your soul's journey. Knowing who you really truly are and what you are really capable of now that you're remembering who you really are as that original soul part of you that is as pure and part of God/ Source and thus connected to everything is the purpose of awakening and using the Akashic Records to do so is their purpose.

Accessing your Akashic Records and just being in them is a very good way to step out of the control of one's ego mind and really step into a place of humility and grace through higher consciousness to All That Is. It is also a great place to just sit in quietly and absorb the high vibration energy as it is healing Divine energy and helps raise your vibration or resonance, thus calms your mind and nervous system like meditation does, allowing you to live your most divinely authentic awakened self.

How the Akashic Records 'Change' Your Life

In general, everything that happens is a personal experience and the view is from that projected perspective. That said, aligning with your soul energies through having your Akashic Records read or working in your own Akashic Records regularly brings enlightened changes to your life further aligning you with your highest and best soul path and maintaining your connection to the Divine/God/Source/All That Is. Those people or things of a different resonance will thus naturally fall away if they don't like the change they sense in you or don't want to face it for themselves and the changes it would bring them. This is a typical fear response as opposed to an embracing love response where they accept you as your now more aligned self. Those in your life coming from a place of fear can often attack from an ego perspective as your light shines and that is ultimately what they too want but the ego feels threatened by this "end" of its reign and will throw a tantrum. The more "far off" one is from their own soul path, or the less aligned one is with the Divine/Source/God/All That Is, or the more scenic route they are choosing to take in life ignoring the signs and discomforts of mishaps, career or life path dissatisfaction, draining relationships, etc., the more extreme the changes can be after Akashic Record work.

Although at a certain point of doing this work regularly the going of that which no longer belongs, or isn't serving your highest and best, or doesn't want to come from a place of love and acceptance, doesn't phase you. All you start to see is what has arrived in its place. All you see is the now Divine dream life you live as synchronicities abound, career is not a thing or series of achievements and money piling but a way of life and that which touches your soul and heart, and relationships are full of love and appreciation and supporting each other's awakening process and living spiritually aligned, a unity consciousness, a New Earth, which is why you are really here.

CHAPTER 4

Akashic Enlightenment Arrives, What Is It?

My Initial Akashic Enlightenment Experience

In March of 2016, about 3 months after the shamanic journey telling me I am to write this book to help others with the Akashic Records and healing, the Akashic Enlightenment Gateway prayer was given to me on March 28th upon opening my Akashic Records with an Arcturian based Akashic Record access prayer I found in a book. Apparently this was what they were guiding me to find so I could receive the Akashic Enlightenment Gateway Prayer. I of course later found out it was Ascended Master Jesus that had used that channel to give me this prayer which is not too surprising considering my previous Angel channeling work and that he was my spirit teacher in my Shamanic Akashic Record work.

When given this prayer I was told to pass it along to all who want it now and in the future as it is key to their enlightenment. That this gateway prayer is not just reading the Akashic Records, but that it is also for life guidance of enlightenment and living a path within that. Thus this prayer is only to be used for someone reading their own Akashic Records for self enlightenment and following their own path along that as best they can.

Now, when I first opened my own Akashic Records with this Akashic Enlightenment prayer, honestly it felt like the heavens had opened and God/Source was in my living room. It definitely caught my attention. I heard one voice very loud, clear and booming instructing me what to do with the prayer. I found out later that that voice was the Lords of the

Akashic Records. At the time, I felt my heart aching and open so much as if pure Divine Love were pouring in. I saw amazing golden light up just above my head and I felt I'd seen God/Source directly above. I was told this prayer was being given to me at this time to help people with the current planetary energy convergences that are occurring at this time, to help guide all that walk the Earth and are ready to go back 'Home' through Ascension to the homeland while still being on Earth. 'Home' here is what is referred to being the inner peace and light within, that each soul is incarnated with, and who tend to forget once in the human body. Home is where your soul rests once it is apart from the body, its programs and knowledge or intelligence, all that is beyond this.

What is Akashic Enlightenment

Akashic Enlightenment allows you to access your own Akashic Records, also known as the Book of Life, for self enlightenment and healing through the 11th density Book of Truth, the Laws of this Universe and beyond, of which your Akashic Records are a part of and which provide the Ascension aspect. By using a 5th density consciousness prayer as your gateway you have access to gain knowledge through the Book of Truth through your soul's record.

Scribed reading of what Akashic Enlightenment is through Akashic Enlightenment:

Akashic Enlightenment: Akashic Enlightenment is for enlightenment, not just reading the Akashic Records. This prayer is beyond the Records. It uses the Records to tap directly into Source as you do in your journeys. This is why it has come to you because you are doing this work on your own in your journeys. Now this is a quicker way for others and you to get there without having to do a journey and go through all the levels you went through to get here. You did the work for everyone else. Now let them walk their paths to enlightenment and let their lives unfold.

Me: Who are you if this isn't just the Records?

Akashic Enlightenment: God/Source/Creator some say Jesus speaks my voice but it is me, God, directly that speaks to you now Sherry through this prayer. As many prayers in the Bible have been created for such, this is doing that in a new way using the Akashic Records energy to spread the message and bring the energy in.

Me: Why do I feel so tired in here?

Akashic Enlightenment: It is of higher vibration than normal Akashic Record reading and it takes getting used to.

Me: Where does the Akashic Enlightenment prayer take you that is the same place I go in my shamanic journeys?

Akashic Enlightenment: 7th Heaven. The place of all souls incarnation. The world of the beyond. Who you were when you were incepted to that place for each person of their own. Their will of who they are is what comes from this place. As you find yourself they too find themselves.

Me: How do I describe that in the book with the Akashic Enlightenment prayer in it?

Akashic Enlightenment: It is the place where their soul was incepted. This is where you were going. This is where this Akashic Enlightenment prayer takes you. From here you can see who you really are, why you are and what you want to do or best serves you in this lifetime as in no other lifetime. It gives you a direct guide to find your true soul happiness and restfulness in the waking world without going to the beyond. It's so you can remember even once you're here and you've forgotten who you are at your root core level while forgetting this causes major bodily disharmonies and wasted soul time or time away from joy. Reconnect with you at your soul level and reconnect with soul joy and love.

Akashic Enlightenment is different from other Akashic Record work by using the Book of Truth. It tells someone their truest soul self as it uses the Laws of the Universe as God intended and NOT altered laws. Altered laws are those in which people have followed lies and their own misbeliefs to create an energy of false laws or truths of your universe which have been creating the false reincarnation cycle on your planet and kept people from proper ascension or returning back to Source as you have done in your shamanic journeys already thus making your Akashic Record experience beyond the places false laws or truths and aligned in the Book of Truth, the Laws of the Universe. The false laws were placed there by those in fear. People who incarnated there. The truths of your world are not the truths of the Universe. They are steeped in fear and lack. They are not true at all.

Me: Who created these?

Akashic Enlightenment: People

Me: Why?

Akashic Enlightenment: For control

Me: Why?

Akashic Enlightenment: Selfishness. Lower resonance. Which is why when you step out of their created lower resonance using this prayer you manifest a new world and new way of being.

Me: Why wouldn't doing regular Akashic Record work that doesn't go through the Book of Truth do this?

Akashic Enlightenment: That's not its purpose. It's purpose is to align you with your soul path. This Akashic Enlightenment with the Book of Truth aligns you with your soul path and brings you or raises you out of the current false system of laws or misbeliefs of your current world to a higher resonance world. Thus why you can meditate in this prayer and it alone will shift you.

Me: How does it do this?

Akashic Enlightenment: By aligning you not only with your soul via your Akashic Records but also with your highest free self outside of this resonance that has many caught in its lies even if they are on their soul path. There still needs to be an energy or resonance upgrade to step out of the current lower vibration of lies. This is ultimate freedom.

So when one asks a question in Akashic Enlightenment the answer will be aligned with their highest soul path as it goes through their Akashic Record AND it will bring transmission alignment in that particular area for their stepping out of the lower vibration of existence on your planet now. Thus doing meditation work in Akashic Enlightenment will bring in transmissions for their highest and best at this time. Asking questions will align them with their highest soul path and bring the necessary energetic transmissions for that area they are actively working on thus raising them to the Book of Truth, True Universal energy, for that subject or area of life.

Akashic Enlightenment is an Akashic Record reading tool AND ascension energy provider via the Book of Truth thus why it is for Self Enlightenment/ Knowledge and Ascension, returning back to Source/ God via the Book of Truth providing the energy resonance of the Truth of the Universe according to God's/Source's Law.

This is our job at the Council of Light and what your Light Language codes align with when you get a transmission. They are from us and a light condensed form of an Akashic Enlightenment reading thus why when you do a reading for someone and use Light Language you see a speed up of all the areas being accessed in the transmissions as it is going at a speed faster than normal language. This ability to see this is from being aligned with the Book of Truth and functioning on the level of the vibration of the Truths of the Universe as Source intended, Love, which is what is encoded in Light Language.

This Love is also what the goal of *A Course In Miracles* is. *A Course In Miracles* is a key to invite one to align with the higher vibration of the Book of Truth as it is limited in its singular and not personalized presentation as Akashic Enlightenment adds the freedom of to do by live reading of your Akashic Records through the Book of Truth on personal areas of struggle. ACIM is the key to the door that is Akashic Enlightenment hence why it was given to you as you were working with it at the time you worked with your Akashic Records. YOU put the two together in this format as intended.

The Akashic Enlightenment Gateway Prayer is a key to open the door for others to be able to access their Akashic Records through the Book of Truth as I was shown and learned how to do in my shamanic journey practice. Through the Akashic Enlightenment Gateway Prayer you'll experience your own Akashic Records, the record of your soul, through the Book of Truth and the Divine wisdom and knowledge of your past, present and future lives. Through this you are helped to understand better why you are here, how your soul is experiencing the ascension process underway at this time, who is helping you in this process and how, clear old energy to help you move along and follow your soul's path of Ascension instead of following outdated or learned patterns, fears, traumas and anxieties. In addition, the healing energy of just being in your own Akashic Records in Akashic Enlightenment also shifts you to a higher vibration or resonance which you will feel upon opening Akashic Enlightenment and which will help you align with who you are at your soul level.

Akashic Enlightenment works with your personal connection to personal enlightenment and ascension through your own Akashic Records using the power of meditation and asking questions to bring instant clarity and manifestation of consciousness to you. Just like a psychotherapist helps navigate upsetting events you experience and uncover the deeper roots of such feelings, the Akashic Records, and a good thorough inquiry on a particular concern, will show to you the truth of the matter be it a forgotten or repressed incident in this life or recorded on the soul level from past lives. This in and of itself will bring you to a higher awareness of who you really are and will teach you how to continue to align yourself in such a manner to your higher soul self, so you can maintain this consciousness and continue it to return back to Source/God/All That Is.

The Akashic Enlightenment Gateway Prayer will work with your full legal name to open your own Akashic Records. Your legally written or documented name represents your vibrational existence in this present time and place.

Note on Densities

Densities as briefly outlined from Akashic Enlightenment and information gathered from the *Law of One* channeled text.

- **12th density:** Council of Light. They give access to the Book of Truth, the truth of this Universe and beyond.
- **11th density:** This density and below are contained in the Book of Truth, the Truth of the Universe and beyond, thus Akashic Enlightenment can help you work up to this level as needed.
- **8th density:** Akashic Records/Book of Life
- **7th density:** end of our creation, lose all identity and memory because merging with awareness of All That Is because there is no more memory, feels like it's all inside of you...after this you are moving out of being a physical human being.
- **6th density:** balanced state of consciousness meaning no longer negative forms of momentum and selfishness is doomed to fail and totally surrendered; your future self being able to access

you; apply wisdom to the love state; The *Law of One* text is a channeling of this density.

- **5th density:** can leave the group consciousness and go solo; things are done astrally; dense vibration; generally considered the love state. Some say that the *A Course In Miracles* text is a channeling of this density.
- **4th density:** start to become more sensitive to all that is around you; begin to remember where you are really from; understanding of death; lose negative oriented path foothold, disappearance of being dishonest as everyone is appeared as you as you have access to other being's consciousness (this is how shamanic divination works).
- **3rd density:** humanity (traditionally); existing more so in ego mind; higher animals/pets, aware they exist by having a name identity and you talk to them and they understand you.
- **2nd density:** plants, animals, minerals
- **1st density:** rocks, dirt, earth

CHAPTER 5

Akashic Aura (Light Language), E.T.'s, and Christ/KRYST Consciousness

First Appearance of Light Language Code

Following my first experiences with using the Akashic Enlightenment prayer, starting as soon as April of 2016, were shifts in my shamanic journeys. Now when I would go to my spirit teacher Teki he would take me to this golden temple in the Upper World and would have me sit on this beautiful strong golden chair or throne in the center of this platform up these stairs, what he called my "Enlightenment Chair".

When I would sit there I would feel the crown of my head heavy with pressure on it and I would feel energy streaming in which I had felt before when I would do Akashic Record work via an access or gateway prayer. I would also see a faint column of light above my head and these symbols, that looked a bit like Mayan or alien glyphs, came in.

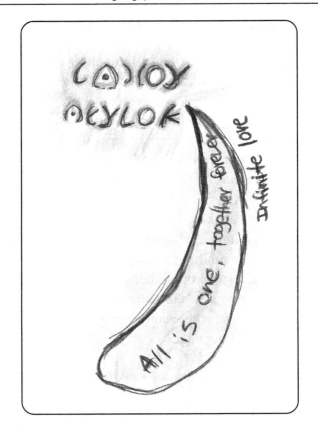

Light Language code and translation which I started
writing after going to Bali in October of 2016.

We did quite a few of these transmissions but it wasn't until later that
I discovered what was really going on then. First, that column is the
same column connected to the soul star chakra and the many higher
chakras above which Ascended Master Jesus had previously activated
in previous shamanic journeys for me, and that secondly it connected
to Akashic Enlightenment and it is one's connection to receiving divine
guidance, wisdom, healing and ascension codes or transmissions. This
time those codes were coming in and I could see them as the Light
Language codes they were just not yet knowing fully what they were
or what they were actually doing, Ascension upgrades, aka aligning my
soul with Source/God/Creation/All That Is.

Mount Shasta Births Speaking Light Language

In August of 2016 I suddenly felt a call to join my shamanic training peer's retreat in Mount Shasta California. It felt like a calling and luckily there was still space. During this retreat we were doing very deep meditation work and receiving higher alignment transmissions and working with the Arcturians, a very peaceful off planet race with a strong focus on enlightenment and who's Akashic Record prayer had brought me the Akashic Enlightenment Gateway Prayer. Also I was regularly using Akashic Enlightenment when walking around the sacred sites there soaking in so much energy through my now well formed upper column of chakras above my head honestly I was quite ungrounded with it all but knew it was part of my experience while there. I would also do brief check ins in my Akashic Records in Akashic Enlightenment in the morning to see what I needed to be focusing on while I was there and amongst those got notice I was going to receive Light Language.

August 11ᵗʰ 2016 Akashic Enlightenment Reading

Me: What do I need to focus on today?

Akashic Enlightenment: Learn Light Language. That is your goal/mission today. It will be given to you later. Then teach others how to do it. It will be part of your Akashic Enlightenment class. But it will be called Akashic Aura Enhancement. It will combine Akashic reading with energy work using Light Language.

I feel later that day is when I received the final transmission to be able to speak Light Language as sure enough come September 27ᵗʰ 2016 came my introduction to speaking Light Language. I wasn't really ready for it despite being told previously I was to learn it so it was a bit odd yet quite powerful!

September 27ᵗʰ, 2016 - Shamanic Journey to the Upper World: Introduction to the Akash, Galactic

Federation, Arcturians, and Speaking Light Language

I put on my headphones and listen to the drumming with my eyes covered and the digital recorder recording. I go up to the Upper World. Archangel Michael shows up and we are in space as soon as I get up there. It's all black with stars sparkling and we stand on an opaque platform.

He tells me I don't need any of the old upper world any more or to merge with the Light Being to come through and I see my old upper world just dissolving and it's just outer space.

To the left is the Akashic Records and to the right is the white door.

Me: Where is here?

Archangel Michael: Here is the higher version of the Akash that holds the Akashic Records and connects to Source.

Me: So I've been journeying to the Akasha

Archangel Michael: To give a definition of that, it is All That Is. The Akashic Record is a person's record within the Akash. These are your new crew members.

He shows Ascended Master Jesus and all the Arcturians standing next to him. And all the angels are here too.

Archangel Michael: This is where you do your healing work now. This is who you are working with now.

Ascended Master Jesus holds me and takes me straight up and to the right and then back down and then straight forward and we're walking forward on this path, it's transparent but everything is black with stars around and you can feel that there are walls that are transparent....like a hallway.

He's telling me to come and he has something to show me. I feel like there is a doorway and he says you've been here before. Oh he's taking me to the Akashic

Enlightenment space. We go through the purple door. Go down and there's the Buddha.

Ascended Master Jesus: Sit and become the Buddha.

I sit and I merge with the Buddha (voice changes lower and calmer). I feel so relaxed. Everything just makes sense. I'm just calm and relaxed and I see everything and I know everything and it's just stillness and oneness.

Ascended Master Jesus: Oneness.

I feel energy coming out of my third eye going up above and splitting down below and I'm turning gold and into the Buddha shape and there's light going up and there's light going down and it's like a....violet ray.

Ascended Master Jesus: This is the Violet Ray of purification. (My voice changes) You are now opening your third eye. And as you open the third eye you open a portal. And through the portal you can walk to other dimensions. All the dimensions that I showed you before.

All these Arcturians show up now pointing at a triangle saying that's what they use, oh this triangle. Ooooh. They're very excited, very excited. They want me to get on their craft.

Ascended Master Jesus: That's ok, it's good to be comfortable learning to work with them.

So I get in the little craft with one. It's a little dark colored saucer with a clear globe on top. We get in and we go through the portal coming out of my third eye. We're going along. Going through. I see this beautiful galaxy below and there's beautiful purple and pink below, like a Milky Way type . I hear an announcement, "Stellar 7587 we've arrived. Docking Sherry Mosley now. Docking Sherry Mosley" and we are at some space station.

Arcturians: You wanted to know about the Galactic Federation so this is what we're showing you.

Me: Well I wanted to know what to do next to live a life aligned with Source.

Arcturians: Well this is what you do to be aligned with Source, you are part of this.

Me: Ok let's go.

This little Arcturian takes my hand. And he's, awww, so gentle, they are so gentle and so sweet. We go and we get on the space station. A Galactic Federation Space Station. And they're all over the universe but he's implying the universe is much bigger than people are aware of right now which is why we had to go through the portal to get here right now. And he takes my hand and swinging me around getting me to come forward.

Arcturian: We don't walk here we just think where we want to be and we just show up. It's teleportation. You just think 'I wanna be there' and boom you're there.

Me: Like if I want to be around the corner then you're there. Ok I get it.

Arcturian: Good, you have to know how to travel like that here so you set your intention of where you want to go and then you're just there.

Me: Ok so where do I want to go?

Arcturian: The gardens.

So we go. Wow. It's this whole beautiful indoor garden. There's this glass up above and it's like a traditional arboretum with white framing around the glass panes. So beautiful. It's just filled with tropical plants. He says they've learned how to synthesize all the light from the stars. Oh he's saying the glass does. When you walk in you're still in the space station but when you walk in it's like a glass wing of the space station so all the glass is actually facing outer space. But it's not just one solid flat piece of glass. They've made it into little panels like you would if you were here on Earth. He explains that the panels collect the star light and sun light from the galaxy and it filters in like the sunlight would for the plants to feed them. And the little white veins or what would be the white framing or caulking around the windows here on Earth are actually like a vine that's a memory or alive and it brings in the energy that the panels absorb so not only does the panel absorb the light to feed the plants but the vine veining.

He's showing, the blue energy goes down along the veining to the back part of the building where it comes down into a simple white fountain of two flat wide basins on top of each other and it goes into the water and they drink the water that has been touched by the sun and he's telling me to drink some, that it heals everything. He says, this is the water that was in the holy grail, this was the water of youth.

And he's smiling and laughing a little saying its not as complicated as humans think it is it's just a complex synthesis of light energy which is what the body needs.

And he says right now you're getting that from your food but the food and the water quality there on Earth is not very high so we're going to start feeding you this water to help you on your galactic mission now that you've accepted it.

He's saying the youthing process will begin now. He's saying now that the Tachyon products I use are similar to this and the silica will help me.

I'm feeling all this.

We're walking up to the fountain and I feel the energy of it already coming through my third eye. And he says because we are in 5D the synthesis of it doesn't just come through your mouth you're taking it in through your third eye. My voice gets quiet and weak as I'm feeling the energy. He's saying the energy of the ...I start taking in deep breaths and breathing heavy. Wow, it's powerful. He's saying I don't need to do my qigong to build my qi I need to just come here because I'm not just building up my subtle body any more I'm building

my etheric body through their dimensional plane to
the fifth dimension absorbing higher nucleus synthesis
through plants. (Sigh, sigh)

Now he's giving me this large tropical looking
bright pink flower with stem and he wants me to eat it.
I'm eating this flower. It tastes really sweet like candy.
He says to eat the whole thing with the green stem as
I was nibbling just the petal. I put it in my mouth and
Ascended Master Jesus steps in and says no no no that's
too much right now just do half of it right now. And the
Arcturian apologizes and says Ascended Master Jesus
is right. And they take half back. I feel a little floaty in
my head and I'm gulping. Whoa my body has this pink
gel around it and I feel buoyant and bouncy. And he
says this is your nucliotosis layer. You need it to walk
around up here now.

And now I'm going to meet the rest of the Federation
and Ascended Master Jesus comes with and we are
walking out to the hallway. We are going to the Council
Room the thought comes in and boom. Whoa. We're
there.

I immediately see this bug face alien, oh he looks
offended I said it like that. He's got a face that looks like
a praying mantis. There's this beautiful oval glass table.
Plants are hanging. They use the plants in a special
synthesis system that comes from the garden into the
galactic station to make it so habitable. The air in here
is just so delicious. And the Arcturian reminds me that
I have to have my pink suite on to be here and he has
me sit down for the meeting.

And wow there is this glowing white being at the
head of the table. Wow there's just so many beings
around the table it would take so long to describe all
of them but they are from all different races. And the
one at the head of the table is this transparent clear, like
the ones in the movie the Abyss. A larger head, quite

wide at the top coming down to a more pointed chin but elongated left to right more than top to bottom. And there are these little electrical veins going through it.

Ok and now they want to start the meeting and I'm quiet. It's like another language, it's like clicks. Oh they want me to speak the language. It's hard. They're saying its Light Language. Makes me a little nauseous trying to say it. I resist and my mouth waters and it feels uncomfortable keeping it in. I start speaking the foreign language...after a bit I start translating some of it in English after speaking the foreign language. There is a private message for me that followed.

Later in other shamanic journeys messages for the masses come through that I record and put up on my YouTube page for them. I also started speaking it spontaneously to myself which I am told are upgrades in the moment for alignment as the energies shift but these came and come from the Council of Light as DNA or cellular alignment transmissions.

Akashic Aura Enhancement/Attunement

After working with Light Language for a while and having some people ask me how I learned how to speak it and how they too can learn to speak it, I did a shamanic journey to ask more about these Akashic Aura Enhancements that are a part of Akashic Enlightenment.

Shamanic journey on Light Language and Aura Enhancement.

I journey to the Upper World to see my Spirit Teacher Horus.

Spirit Teacher Horus: (Draws Light Language codes in the sand.) This is from your ancient lineage Mayan lifetimes. You were given the codes back then so you can do it now. He reminds me how I was shown this in an Akashic Record reading about my soul's path already. This is your lineage. This is who you are. Your soul remembers.

He opens a portal and takes me through to that lifetime. It's a jungle. He's showing me the Akashic Reading I did before as I remember this image from that reading. I see Mayan pyramids. Steps. There is a symbol for Horus that is also there. A creature with a bird head. He's showing me the temple. Pointing to it that that's where you get it from. I was a child that grew up in the jungles. But some sort of princess, wearing white gowns, like a sorcerous. I had abilities. He's showing me I'd move my hands and this light would come from them. And all the animals would come to me and talk to me. I could control the elements. It was a form of what you'd call shamanism. He says I was aligned with Source energy then so I was able to change the elements and commune with animals. I did a lot of powerful rituals. I'm also seeing the eye that's in Egypt. He's saying that these are the same origins. The Mayan lifetime is connected to the Egyptian lifetime. He's showing me that there's a chair or throne I'd sit in. I had a royal position. The chair that Teki had me sit in to receive the light codes in previous journeys is the same chair I'd sit in in that lifetime. Teki had brought it through in a more Buddhist Enlightenment perspective showing me that they are all the same. Be it Enlightenment, be it Mayan shamanism or Egyptian ancient rituals. They all go to the same place and all of them are the roots to your lineage of Light Language. In all those areas I was connecting to Source energy and it gave me my ability to speak Light Language.

Me: What is Light Language and the dialect I speak?

Spirit Teacher Horus: It's not so much a dialect as it is how someone's soul resonates and the sounds come out. It's related to your soul imprint in connection to

Source and that's what creates the sound of your Light Language because it's coming through your soul.

Me: What else can you tell me?

He's showing me this Mayan lifetime and in the air there are these glowing codes that look somewhat like Mayan glyphs but he says it's Light Language.

Spirit Teacher Horus: If you want you can look at your Mayan lifetime as being connected to your Pleiadian times if you want to look at it that way.

Me: What are the Akashic Aura Enhancements?

Spirit Teacher Horus: You're already doing them. When you do the Light Language in the Akashic Enlightenment readings these are Akashic Aura Alignments. It's a cellular aura. It's not the traditional aura that people think of. As you bring in the Light Language you shift the cellular aura to a higher life form. Thus it's called Akashic Aura. When you combine the Light Language with teaching Akashic Enlightenment it makes it more of an attunement. This accelerates the persons attunement.

For now I am offering Akashic Aura Enhancements or Attunements to bring forth your own Light Language abilities in one on one Akashic Enlightenment with Light Language session attunements which may eventually expand to classes.

Light Language and Christ/KRYST

First, remember that KRYSTAL represents the first sounds of creation, KA RA YA SA TA LA. Notice they were sounds. This would lead to creation being created and/or altered via sound. Thus the language of God/Source/All That Is is sound. God/Source/All That Is would be considered the original 'Light' thus Light Language is the language of Source/Creation/God/All That Is thus a language of Divine Love. This is why it exists and furthermore why it can bring vibrational alignment through the vibration of sound as DNA upgrades and cellular healing to return one back to this Original Creation Consciousness, KRYSTAL, as it is connected to sound resonance, vibration.

The Bible refers to Light Language as speaking in tongues which is said to be when someone is filled with the Holy Spirit. The Holy Spirit is also referred to as the Shekinah in many Jewish texts and is considered the left hand side of God. At one point I was shown and told by Archangel Metatron that I now sit at the left hand of God. This would appear to be the Divine Feminine which is what most religions early on cut out of organized religions in order to gain power and control of the people by cutting them off from their own divine connection to the Holy Spirit for divine guidance and healing and ascension of their own. Hence why at that time anyone with such divination abilities was called a witch or sorcerer and killed. If people got the idea that communing with 'spirits' or the divine was possible and helpful the governments and organized religions would lose control, power and money. So this natural and God given right of divine connection and ability to speak tongues is a blessing and sign of connection to the Holy Spirit, Christ/ KRYSTAL Consciousness and is a form of Divine Healing.

This is further shown in the *The Book of Knowledge: The Keys of Enoch* text. (Hurtak p. 238) It talks about how this Language of Light was originally a part of humanity but through the misuse of these abilities and more in genetic manipulation from beings of higher consciousness, humans were made to forget who they truly are in order to became a slave race created to look for gold as they sought it for it's pure conduit abilities (that is actually from the *12th Planet (Book 1): The First Book of the Earth* by Zecharia Sitchin) or other "chores" of this other race. These beings misusing such consciousness and higher powers were intervened upon by the higher Councils of Light who basically altogether cut humans off from these higher sources that were being misused to manipulate them into being slaves to keep them from communicating with these beings and breeding with them. In the *A Course In Miracles* text this would be referred to as "the separation". (Schucman T-2.I.2.) "These related distortions represent a picture of what actually occurred in the separation, or the 'detour into fear'. 2 None of this existed before the separation, nor does it actually exist now. 3 Everything God created is like Him. (T-2.I.3.) 5 What is seen in dreams seems to be very real. 6 Yet the Bible says that a deep sleep fell upon Adam, and nowhere is there reference to his waking up. 7 The world has not yet experienced any comprehensive reawakening or rebirth." And this "separation" is why the *A Course In Miracles* book was created to again align one with their Christ/KRYST mind outside the confines of organized religion as well as how one seeks to acquire Boddhisattva Enlightenment, or being a spiritually awakened being, in Buddhism. As well as the story of Sophia, the goddess of Wisdom, speaking of the fall from infinite divine light, as well as the path of enlightenment as a return to the Divine.

Only once humans are able to again align with their original Christ/ KRYST Consciousness, Divine Light, Enlightenment, would one be able to again have access to Light Language. Thus Light Language is seen as an immediate connection with the Creator/God/Source/Elohim used to code knowledge, or Divine Knowledge as it is better known in the *A Course In Miracles* text. A language of creation with "knowledge from a core memory of information being shared by the higher spiritual levels of existence, allowing man to read the 'records of the mysteries' in the higher heavens" thus "affecting the psychological, neurological, biochemical and cosmological levels of thought-attunement". (Hurtak p. 585) Since this Language is Universal it can also be used to communicate with other planetary beings and "enables the Lords of Light to reach many planetary worlds and reality levels simultaneously, and fuse the different languages into the same scenario abstracts". (Hurtak p. 585)

Now, the Council of Light are the ones bringing in the Book of Truth for Akashic Enlightenment here now in this book as a written form of the same consciousness as the Light Language or Christ/KRYSTAL Consciousness ascension and alignment healing. It is the active live version of what the *A Course In Miracles* text, as well as other Christ/ KRYST consciousness texts or modalities, provides the key to due to the Book of Truth access.

CHAPTER 6

Council of Light Brings The Book of Truth, the Laws/Truths of This Universe and Beyond

Who Are The Council of Light?

In a shamanic journey I was told that the Council of Light is God Creation energy in the purest accessible form and is life's non-incarnated beings and ascended beings who incarnated back and who thus have the lesson on how to teach this. Included in the Council of Light are Ascended Masters Buddha and Jesus. There are many other saints and holy teachers there as well. That's why they are able to teach these processes.

Also, according to the *The Book of Knowledge: The Keys of Enoch* text the Council of Light includes a few specific councils with their own tasks or assignments.

> **Councils of Light** - The Councils of Nine, Twelve, Twenty-Four, One Hundred and Forty Four, One Hundred and Four Thousand governing this galaxy and other regions of distant universes (The Kuchavim). The "Councils of Light" should not be confused with solar and planetary councils which are ephemeral.
>
> **Council of Nine** - Tribunal of Teachers governing our immediate super-galactic and galactic region,

subject to change in evolving 'new programs' of the Father's Kingdom.

Council of Twelve - Sons of Heaven working with God (Source) to supervise the creation and regeneration of the lower worlds.

Council of Twenty-Four - Council governing spiritual civilizations in the Son universe which is not to be confused with the Twenty-Four elders.

Council of One Hundred and Fourty-Four Thousand - Tribunal of Ascended Masters administering the Programs of 'the Ancient of Days' the Infinite Mind working through Yaweh as Creator God. The Hierarch of the 'higher heavens' that governs the hierarchies of the midheavens and lower-heavens, judging the final 'soul programs' of man and Master alike.

(Hurtak p. 571)

Introduction to the Council of Light

In February of 2017 after teaching a few of the Akashic Enlightenment group classes and upon visiting the University of Pennsylvania Museum of Archaeology and Anthropology Egyptian section, I received some transmissions of divine keys and codes while there in Akashic Enlightenment. Those transmissions started a new phase of my shamanic journeying introducing me first to the Council of Light and then the Book of Truth as the Egyptians had the same access themselves. I had downloaded the divine code or key of this while at the museum due to being in Akashic Enlightenment while there.

Shamanic journey introducing me to the Council of Light.

I go to Upper World and see my usual Universe of black space and stars. I see Egyptian pyramids in the background in a sandy desert and UFOs above them. My spirit guide Metatron points to go towards the

pyramids. I go and step into the sand. I meet with my
new spirit teacher Horus who had shown up earlier in
January 2017. We sit in the sand. Horus is across from
me and an ET on either side of me creating a circle of
the 4 of us.

Me: Who are they?

Spirit Teacher Horus: Your ET family companions.
Your guides. Although while I'm here I am your guide.
They are facilitating the connection. They are calling
me in for you.

Me: What do you mean by my ET guides?

Spirit Teacher Horus: You have an ET lineage to
the Pleiadians. That's what brings you here to Egypt.

Now he's doing something to my third eye from
his. I feel my head getting confusing and full. I feel the
crown of my head opening. He's pushing through my
third eye to open my crown. I'm twitching. I see all this
code. Looks like Light Language symbols coming down
into my head and then it closes.

Spirit Teacher Horus: You're receiving new codes to upgrade you DNA. The code we gave you now will help you move forward.

Me: Ok can you explain more?

Spirit Teacher Horus: The light codes you downloaded at the museum were the memory of being there and that is what you are here to be doing now in this lifetime and what you are reinitiating in this lifetime. This is your primary work. You downloaded what your primary work is to do. The work will unfold.

I'm standing there in the sand with Metatron and Horus. I see all the ETs above and feel weird. Horus asks if it would make me feel better to know that they are Pleiadians and I say yes I guess it does. He takes me into the pyramid that was in the sandy desert behind him. Horus has me standing in the center. There's a podium. He's adjusting my chakras and opens the rainbow beam of light out of the crown of my head. I see and feel the ETs circling around us in the pyramid now. Horus says to just see them as Pleiadians. They're assisting the connection. I see the white light they are sending to the center going to the center of the pyramid we are all standing in.

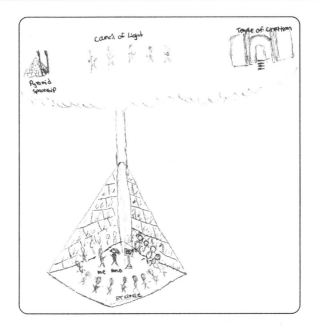

Horus and I start to go up the center of the pyramid in the white light. Horus reminds me to relax. Out of the top of pyramid to the level where everything is peace and quiet and I just want to stay here. I feel them pulling me up and calling me up. I feel scared. I don't see Horus and call out to him and realize he's already up there and trying to pull me up there. I go up. The energy is so much lighter here. So much love. So much better here. Omg. There's just so much love and I just feel my heart expanding so much. They're trying to take my hand and now my left hand is moving on its own. I don't know what's happening. They're saying I'm having trouble holding this level of energy and to just focus and let go.

They're leading me now to some sort of temple. It's gold. It's an Egyptian pyramid. I don't understand. We are in the sky and there's a pyramid here as well. It's a smaller one. Human sized. It's almost hard to see this. Such a different resonance. There's all these Light Beings. And Horus is telling me I'm with the Council of Light right now. It's a very high vibration. They're holding the space for you to do this work. I feel so different and nervous.

Now they have me sit in the pyramid. It's a spaceship. And as I sit inside it's gold and it has all these hieroglyphics on the outside and these two pointed staffs in front of it. And it glows gold with white energy around it. It feels so familiar.

Council of Light Beings: This is how you used to travel in time and space when you were in Egypt don't you remember?

Me: It does it feels very familiar.

I see the Buddha sitting inside. This represents the enlightened state it takes to get here. They tell me to relax. I sit in the pyramid and it lifts up and goes somewhere. I don't know what's happening. It's hard to breath. They wonder if I'm ready. I feel like I'm in a deep meditative state now. They help adjust my energy. I'm twitching. The pyramid takes me going and we're going. Traveling in time. Traveling in time. I am in two places at once. Traveling in time. I dunno where they are sending me.

Council of Light Beings: To see the future you are building.

I see the pyramid that I'm in. I've come to some place. It's all dark but the energy I feel is so high vibration. So loving. I want nothing else but that. And the Council of Light Beings are kind of back saying, good that's all she needs for now. Now that you've touched it and accepted it you need to go receive it. I'm sent to go get a transmission and end up doing a Light Language download and then end the journey.

That Light Language message was a message for the world of the coming changes that the Eclipse of August 2017 was bringing and it is up on my YouTube page in that form.

Upon my next shamanic journey to the Council of Light, I go in the time travel pyramid to a temple known as the Temple of Creation, where the Akashic Records/Book of Life are and the Book of Truth. This is where I get my first download or transmission of the Book of Truth text as lessons and chapters. Each time I return they give me more chapters and lessons that I ultimately scribe post shamanic journey and some come spontaneously when I sit to write and they know that I am ready to write what they, the Council of Light, send.

After these journeys and upon a little research I found that my spirit teacher Horus is often referred to as another form of Christ and according to *The Book of Knowledge: The Keys of Enoch* text the Eye of Horus is known to be used by the Masters and Lords of Light as "a template of vibratory patterns to generate physical creation" or "divine creation coordinating the minds of the Elohim (God) so that the divine image can be passed on to all 'generations of creations'". (Hurtak p. 575) Thus why Horus as my spirit teacher plus the codes I downloaded at the museum end up being what bring me to the Council of Light and ultimately to the Book of Truth/Truths of the Universe/Cosmic Laws in the Temple of Creation where the Elohim are using this to encode new Creation energy or shifts for me to share with others.

Council of Light Introduce The Book of Truth

According to the Council of Light and Akashic Enlightenment, the Book of Truth is timeless and universal and is the big library of which your Akashic Records are but one hallway of. It contains the Laws of the Universe, our singular Universe and beyond, and God Creation as they truly are free of human interpretation and scientific theories and laws that are untrue bias or forms of ego upon God's/Source's Will or one's True Will which is the same as God's/Source's Will once one aligns once again with their True Will via the soul.

Once one knows the laws that are governing the True Universe and understand it that is how you step out of your false law Universe binary self loop of being within itself and moving to connecting with All. The Book of Truth is the exit point out of the singular universe to the greater larger True Universe at large.

In another shamanic journey I was shown a bubble around our universe as most see it. The Council of Light shares that the powers that be in your world told everybody a certain amount of laws that are untrue and even hide the True Laws of your Universe from you. This is why you have to learn first the laws of your singular universe so you can step out of it into the larger encompassing universe which is normally how it's supposed to be. This is why it's the Book of Truth. It's the book of how the universe actually is of your singular universe and everything outside of it.

The Book of Truth downloads I've received are the Laws and Lessons of how the Universe functions. Some of these I have started scribing to share but have been told that the chapters and lessons in it are best taken in when they are personally applied to your current situation via accessing your Akashic Records through Akashic Enlightenment rather than reading it as a text. It is a massive database like the Akashic Records thus it is best to have an intention to apply it to for best results.

That said, to get an example of the Book of Truth library or database your personal Akashic Enlightenment readings and meditations will pull through, here is what I have scribed thus far of some of what I have received. The Council of Light has told me it may not make much sense until you have access to the entire Book of Truth, in this case, via using Akashic Enlightenment.

CHAPTER 7

Book of Truth, Volume 1, via the Council of Light

This chapter is completely scribed from multiple transmissions received in shamanic journeys to the Council of Light.

* * *

This is not a prewritten script, this is just the truth as it is now. This world you see before you is not the real world. It is a world that was created a long time ago before all existed. This is a hard concept to take in one drop, thus we are giving it to you in small drops. The WE is us, the Council of Light, here to help with humanity's Ascension. It is time and it is now. Do not hesitate to accept this now. It is imperative that you cooperate and take in this light for all else will be needless suffering. This is our message through Sherry for the Book of Truth Volume One.

Book of Truth Vol 1, Chapter/Lesson 1: What is Love? Why is Love?

Love is the existence of the All. The All that is within each of you naturally. You are Love. Love is you. There is nothing outside of Love thus there is nothing outside of you. This is the natural law of All That Is. This has been forgotten for centuries, lifetimes, eons, place whatever time you want on it but there is no time so it just feels as pain for you for that is all it truly is. A separation in your mind and your heart from your soul from your God/Source.

The truth of Love is that it always exists and always has. Why? No one really knows. It is a force unto it's own. What is not known at this time is that IT is creation itself. Love is creation. This has been lost for a long time and is coming back to realization now on this planet at this "time". This knowledge is coming to you now to show you that the truth has always been there you just didn't know it so let it be.

Accept this truth and all will be one and right with you and your God who is you. You are Love and Light and God and All That Is all at once in one time for there is only one time at one time always. There is only a disconnection from this time and the realization that Love is All That Is. There is a reason that is a saying and a song. Don't think about the reason just see that it is and that there are no mistakes.

Love does not sustain you, it be you. You are love. Love and you are one in of the same. When you learn this your pain and the universe as you know will cease to exist. This is the truth. Look around you and see that others are too in this place.

What is love?
Love is all.

Now why is love.

Because Love is creation. It always has been. Nothing has been true. There is no "creator" there is only Love. That is what God is and what is creation. Love. That is it. Thus when you align with Love you are God and you create. That is all there is. Nothing else is true. That is how all came to be. Love. Then all pain is the fall from Love.

Imagine a globe, a ball.

Hold in your left hand. Pass it to your right hand. Now what created that idea to do that? How did that come to be? Your desire which is a form of Love to see it and experience it in another place in another way. Some call this manifestation but that is still a limited view. What it is is Love. Love generates this and creates this. Love is desire and Desire is

Love. They are the same. So align with Love and thus align with Desire and this is true "life" and form and creator of form. Love.

Book of Truth Vol 1, Chapter/Lesson 2: Truth of Faith

Faith is a belief of the fallen. Those that have fallen are the truth seekers to believe again in what they have fallen from. What this truly takes is Love to find faith to seek the desire to follow the faith of Love again. There is no other faith. This is what is meant when it is said to follow a false faith. It is not that there are other "gods" but other faiths that are not of the true faith.

So what is the true faith.

True Faith is the faith in Love. For Love is all there is. If you truly have Faith in Love all falls in life and in line with God for God is Love for God is Faith and God is creation of All That Is. So if you have Faith you have Love. But having Faith in Love is the ONLY Faith there is now. There is but this one Faith. To follow other is to follow other "gods", as the bible once refereed to having or following or believing in "other gods" that just means losing your Faith in Love, your true creator, your true God which is you as the love that is you. That is the only Faith. All religions stray from this. This is why the Council of Light has decided at this time to tell you of the true Faith and only Faith of existence, the root and core Faith, for there is only one and has always only been one.

Take an island for example. Believe that you see an island in the middle of the ocean. Now see yourself on a boat floating through that ocean. You look up in the sky and see all the stars. You seek guidance here, though the island is within sight just before you. Why do you look up to seek guidance when the island of truth sits right before you? Lack of Faith. If you had true Faith you would see what is already right in front of you. True Faith. Once you have that true Faith you return to the only island that is paradise and that is the paradise because you got there with Faith and not looking up for other guidance. Faith brings you to paradise for it is based on Love and Love is all creation, Love is God.

So hold true Faith and do not stray. Look before you and see the truth already right in front of you for there is no other so there is no need to search for another and this is the ONLY truth of Faith.

Book of Truth Vol 1, Chapter/Lesson 3: What is a Lie?

A lie is that which is a false belief. Close to that of lack of Faith but it is a belief that is not true. It holds a resonance of that which isn't Love, thus it isn't creation and thus it isn't. Now because its energy truly isn't when it is believed as true it causes pain for in its energy it holds emptiness and this is felt as a lack of connection to anything real, a separation, for it is for it holds no Truth or Love or creation. It is a dead end. It is dead energy. When you move forward on your path soon you will feel a lie as it holds no energy for you to create with thus you will not even notice it or see it, it wont cross your path because you are so much pure Love and creation energy it can not exist in your existence because it holds no energy and is literally a void thus it wont exist. Thus anyone existing in lies will cease to exist in your presence and reality and world. This is quantum physics. You can not have a not in a real. What we mean is you can not have a vacuum in nothingness. When there is nothingness there is nothing for nothing to exist. Thus they will cease to exist. That is what is happening now as more align with Love. As more align with Love, lies and nothingness begin to cease to exist.

A lie is a void and holds nothing. Thus it is nothing.

(A personal note to me in this transmission I thought I'd share: Just as The Nothing in the movie Never Ending Story came to destroy everything it ceased to exist when she (the princess) was given a new name because a new creation, out of Love, was given and thus The Nothing couldn't exist any more.

Book of Truth Vol 1, Chapter/Lesson 4: Lies Create Holes

Lies create holes in time and space. Then there is a lie that creates a hole or a gap in time and space. For all time is all the time this creates a hole or rip in time for it is not real. It is nothingness. When there is a hole in time and space it creates a gap in time. These gaps in time are where "people" fall. So when you feel you've lost someone that you knew that is because they've fallen into a hole that is created by a lie. Now that is why you must align with Love for as you align with Love the lie ceases and this sews up the fabric of time to create a seamless tapestry again thus making the universe whole again. As a person makes the universe whole again it perpetually creates more from this point for now there is a stabler point from which to create. This is what is meant by aligning oneself with Soul/Source/God/All That Is. For that is what is real and that is the ONLY place you can truly create from as all else is just a side line or rip in fabric that waves around in the wind till you sew it back together again. That is why it is a waste of time or energy or a loss of energy or time that you do this. It is not aligned with Love/God/Creation and thus you are choosing it as part of your separation of believing inserting that which IS NOT the truth of the universe.

Now how did these even come exist. This is the part that is most confusing to you at this time. If all is Love and Creation how do these lies even exist that create holes? They are your choice. You are given free will choice to choose the fabric and how it is written and creating from Love from here or you can create your own tapestry. When you create your own tapestry though you are literally in your own world then and not a part of the Collective. You have taken a side detour to learn something of your own. This is not wrong or bad but it is a lie in the sense that it is NOT the Truth of the Universe. Thus we are telling you at this time so you can choose to do it or not.

Now for those who have been doing this for a long time not knowing that they are creating and living in a world that is a lie and not the True Universe have some unwinding or repairing of the fabric of time to get back to what IS the Truth.

That is why we are telling you this now so you can fast forward this process now to be relieved from the slow painful way of doing this now. It is as simple as walking away and aligning in Love. Love heals all. This is why Ascended Master Jesus came to show this. It was a pure example of what it is to align with Love. Now we know this is a lot and it is confusing at this time but this is the Truth of the Universe which you agreed to know at this time.

Book of Truth Vol 1, Chapter/Lesson 5:
True Creation Through Love

Once one is aligned in Love and out of ego is when True Creation begins to form again. That of the true dream state of the Divine Universe of the Divine Law of Attraction due to Love as a state of True Creation as it is God as you are God. Once you are in this surrendered state the God Universe of yourself opens unto you and you are truly free to join in the fabric of the All That Is the Universe that is and is connected to God and the Godhead of it's true valid creation ability and power of which you were originally incarnated into to. This is the step all beings are attempting to get back to at this time. This is the original connection that was lost.

A place of True Creation as related to the Original Godhead/Source/Creation. From here is where higher intelligences operate from. They have rejoined this consciousness level and free flowing form of connection to the Godhead. Once they have, this opens endless possibilities. The endless possibilities is what the ego mind fears for it renders it totally and completely useless which is where you are heading now.

This lesson states that no matter can exist without connection to the Godhead thus any and all matter is connected to the Godhead and it is a matter of returning to True Love and thus creation and thus back to True Self which reconnects to their True Will power of being as a being of God and part of God. This is daunting in the small reality currently present on Earth as it is and it is what is being returned to at this time and place. This is why this book is coming in now. It is now time to see past the veil that has even been accepted as the limited truth. It is now time for the real Truth of the Universe as it is present at this time and space so it can too be transcended which is the grander plan of All That Is at this time and in all time in all time of all times present past and future.

Do not fear you will not be alone in this path and it will be clearly unveiled to you upon the next following 3 chapters of aligning within in your own Godhead as you are.

Book of Truth Vol. 1, Chapters/Lessons 6, 7, 8: A Trilogy of the Truth of Alignment

This is not a singular process but a group process and calling of the larger soul collective to join in the oneness that they are. Through this connection reconnection to God is once made again and followed within. This text will now bring you to this alignment in its ingestion from text to mind through reading as a thought present as energy coming to you now.

First off know that this is the Truth of the Universe as it is. It is no longer a falsity to believe this or take this in. This is the first step of your realignment. Secondly, take a breath and realize there is more than what is going on in this present moment for you now. Take a look outside yourself as you presently are and place yourself outside this room, this space, this planet, this galaxy. Good. Now you see you are a part of a grander Universe.

Now from here read this text from the Book of Truth as an alignment text. This text is to be spoken out loud for your own alignment:

> *This is a time of truth that I now live. This is the only truth I have ever known or will know or have known for all time is one and all time is true as one as God created it and created us.*

> (Us is the unit of measure of reality of the Universal and also Global Consciousness of the masses as you know them now.)

That was it. That was the shift. It is not as hard as you may think it is and only requires a surrender and a truth for you to smoothly just let your energy slide into this realignment.

Situating with Your Realignment

Now that you are realigned it is time to situate yourself to it. This is not as hard or complicated as you are now thinking.

Take a breath in and slowly let it out with your eyes closed. Feel your feet on the floor or Earth beneath you. Know that you are a larger part of the Cosmos now at large, this is all all this beyond your Universe and galaxy. See it as the Universal Truth. Now know that God is leading you on this path back to your own salvation of Truth of your Universe as it is by the Book of Truth of which there is only one True Universal law that applies to you and to any and all. Now knowing this Universal Truth of the Book of Truth you are now freed of any and all misconceptions beyond this, at this time, past time and all time hence forth for now is the time to see the Book of Truth as it truly is to you.

This is the second realignment now complete.

Knowing You're Realigned

Now it is time to step forth on your path as realigned with your personal Book of Truth as you know it. Now this is where things will differ for each of you individually as an individual aspect or soul part of God and All Creation at this time, past time and all time hence forth for now is the time for your personal Book of Truth Soul Realization to step forth within you and thus you on your own path as a being connected to the greater consciousness of the Earth and Universe and Universal Truths known as the Book of Truth.

Your Angels and guides will take it now from here for you. Look for signs and follow your intuition as you move forward on your path at this time, past time and all time hence forth for now you walk in the knowing of your Book of Truth alignment. So it is. Amen.

(Flower of Life picture to assist in this alignment over all and its reactivation at this time.)

Book of Truth, Vol. 1: The Tale of Two Cities Long Lost

One city was majestic and clear and the other city was foggy and lost. It was a tension between two sides of a universal switch and change of which no one knew which to choose as true light is masked between the two. So some went to live in one city while others still went to the other city. Dark and light seemed to be the two choices.

Then one day a man came through and walked up the river that run between the two different cities. He asked them why do they force themselves to choose when the mountain of love, abundance and All That Is is just beyond the river if you follow the flow of it home. Take the river home and it will lead you to a place where you do not need to choose any longer. In no longer having to choose there is peace within and calm with that and happiness and joy like you've never experienced. So follow me.

Some people were just curious and followed him into the river and walked behind him not really knowing what journey they were embarking on but were tired of feeling like their life was nothing but constant choice between all the same things.

He led those that followed to a large rock in the river. This is the pillar of doubt he said pointing to it. See how the water gets stuck here around it and gets dirty and other little rocks build up around it as well as dirt and leaves. He asked them to help him move the rock out of the river to the bank from where it slid down from. Once they did that they watched as the water flowed through clearing all the dirt and dead leaves. They continued on their journey up the river.

Now they came to a tree with a branch extending over the river. Majestic and strong was this tree, full and alive and so many leaves it was abound with life and Source energy. Still in the river the man points to the branch up above his head a few feet and pulls it down. He says, use this to help cross this area as the river runs fast here and could knock you down if you don't take support from this tree branch. So one by one they accepted the support from the tree branch and made it through the faster rougher waters. The man says, those trees love to help and are always around so never hesitate to look for them.

Now further down the river they go. This time they stop at a pool. It was clear and calm and the birds were chirping and the water sparkled clearly. Here is where we drink and rest he said. Always remember to rest and drink and take care on your journey when the time to rejuvenate comes. So they all drink the water and lay down on the river bank next to the pool to nap. Before long they realized they were dreaming fantastic dreams.

In these dreams they were already at the end of their journey. They'd made it to the great mountain the man spoke of. It was the land of milk and honey as fresh food was abound from fruit trees, to live stock, to chicken eggs and fish and grains. There was a community already here living in great abundance with plenty to share. The group was so happy to have arrived they immediately partook in the bountiful feast their new family offered them. After this they awoke from the dream expressing the fantastic dream each of them had to each other realizing they'd all had the same dream. But how is that possible one of them asked the man. Because you are already there he said.

And that is the Tale of Two Cities Long Lost.

Book of Truth Vol. 1, Chapter/Lesson 9: The Darker States

To believe a lie is to believe a falsity of God thus it is not true as it is not aligned with Love, thus when you believe this lie your "fate" shall change to adjust with the lie so that the lie is undone to be so painfully experienced that you either release it or live in it's present hell. This hell state is the darker side. Now with God there is no dark or light and thus this appeared hell's equal opposite side of light is still not that of true love as aligned with God thus it is still not not believing in the lie but merely showing you the other side to allow escape granted by seeing it for what it is. Most get caught in the parallel worlds of dark and light believe in one or the other when neither is actual true alignment with God/Source/All That is. That is the one has given up both for the center line, the Truth of both dissolved together often referred to as Dharma Theory. Where the two lines merge as one. The ONE is the one as you know it and who you know yourself to actually be. There is only one ONE, thus ANYTHING outside of that is a lie not in the sense of a lie but in the sense of light or dark, both being lies.

**Book of Truth Vol. 1, Chapter/Lesson 10:
How to Ascend These (Darker States)**

This is actually a very simple matter that is mostly overlooked or more misunderstood. You don't even need dark or light to go beyond them. You can choose to immediately just go beyond either by following that Law of Love. What is the Law of Love?

First we must go over the the Law of One.

The Law of One is that all are equal thus there is ONLY one ONE. There is you and only you. Thus anything is part of the ONE, the ONE which is thus God as you are God. Thus if you are God thus the lie is false and the light and dark are false as neither are part of the actual Law of One. Law of One states that only alignment with Love is true Law of One and God only lives by the Law of One, you. You are God and God is you. There is only one. Grasp this and all will be forgiven.

The Law of Love is that all have already been forgiven as seen before and after God has created as God has created all thus God is Love and Love is God and so are too Love and God. This is the Law of Love. Now if you are God and God is Love then there is no 'dark" thus taking this in is the only forgiveness needed to understand how there is no "darker state" thus this alone will ascend such a belief for that is all a darker state is, a misbelief, also previously spoken of as a lie. Once you know it is a lie that will collapse it's existence for as we said before a lie does not really exist for it is a hole. Thus it sews back up and there is no more "darker state".

Book of Truth Vol. 1, Chapter/Lesson 11: Forgiveness

To forgive another is to forgive yourself. This you know and understand. What is not seen is what happens on the larger scale from such an act. As one forgives another it undoes the lie that was understood to be true. As this is done each party is freed from the lie that was holding them in that stuck and certain believed place that was actually false. Since they see that it is not that other's True Being and see that it is a lie and forgive the lie, its emptiness is then sacrificed as a whole and it implodes. One may react in fear to such an occurrence but that is not necessary and it is merely the shift that is affecting them now as they are now freed from this lie they were putting themselves into to begin with. Once freed and allowed to accept they will then follow a higher path. This is what is known as the resurrection. It is a forgiveness of following the lie that was never true and rising out of it. That is it. When many of these are done at a time as exampled by Christ you can reach an unparalleled level of forgiveness that is beyond the human mind while in the body. This is the embodiment of the Christ energy and is ultimate forgiveness.

Book of Truth Vol. 1, Chapter/Lesson 12: Memories

Memories are that which are beyond the ego mind and back to Source. Now this is confusing to many as back to Source would most normally be out of memories altogether, however, because Source is actually comprised of every memory and IS every memory, all memories lead back to Source thus it all depends which ones you choose to follow. If you follow darker memories you will follow that path back to Source. If you follow loose and flowing memories you will follow that back to Source. If you follow love memories you will follow that back to Source. Thus the road is your free will of which you will experience what you 'want' to experience. What you want is created by which memories you are activating now in the present to get to where you are going. To make Active Dreaming Memories is another way of Higher Memories not yet experienced in that time and place and beyond your current incarnation and allowing you to more readily tap into what would be considered your Soul Memories thus higher than just experience alone and thus closer to Source as it is closer to your Soul thus making it a Higher Memory or a Dream Memory. Following Dream Memories are the best way to go for they are of a higher energy.

Book of Truth Vol. 1, Chapter/Lesson 13: A New Beginning

Now what is meant by a new beginning Here is not what is meant by a new beginning there. A new beginning is a reset to a Higher Memory. When you reset to a Higher Memory you are following a higher plane, or timeline as many call it, and it then is thus free of many of the tangles of the old incarnated memory laden path. To get a new beginning one must step out of the lies of the current incarnation that have been learned as to be true and surrender to the Higher Dream Memory or Soul Alignment, Soul Memory that attaches you back to your highest path back to Source. This is the ideal now and what is vastly available and of which many do not fully understand and just know it is happening. This is because they are not conscious of the Dream Memory they are going back to. To become conscious of the Dream Memory you are going back to or that you WISH or WANT to go back to is a process known as Ultimate Dream Regression. This is accomplished through Akashic Enlightenment through an Ultimate Dream Regression Access session in which one looks at what is their Ultimate Dream of their soul at this time, outside of all incarnated memories. This will show them this new "timeline" they are wishing to jump to at this time as they are ready to move beyond what they took as "real" over all. It is an accelerated time leap and what an Akashic Enlightenment session and healing can do when one is ready to let go of, surrender, the incarnated memory for the Dream Memory. Most are ready who find this now, so go now and embark on your Highest Ultimate Dream Memory.

CHAPTER 8

Book of Truth Scripture, Time of Change: Lessons of Ascension, via the Council of Light

(Ascension Mastery School)

This chapter is completely scribed from a transmission of "scripture" received in a shamanic journey in which I was asked by Archangel Metatron (who encodes or maintains the Akashic Records) to receive for putting in this book and given by the Council of Light. Upon getting this message from Metatron I was also shown an image of the pyramid I usually use in my journeys to travel up to the Council of Light. In this image the pyramid was on fire and in flames at the very top of it with a dove flying above and Metatron telling me "they are burning Divinity". Following is the transmission I received. (Scripture used here is a term for sacred writing.)

* * *

This is the truth as it is now. This is not a prewritten script. This is the Laws of the Universe now, as it is now and so it is written. This is a channel for the book the Book of Truth of the times of change to come.

This is a time of change as many know as are wondering why this change is happening now. It is because it is ordained in highest order to be so. It is a confusing time because many have not been told so by the prearranged channels that were to initiate them as promised. The channels have been compromised in greed, lust and selfishness. Thus we are finding other channels to bring you what they were to bring to you as promised. This is their choice we go around now.

The truth of the times is that the Ascension Mastery School has not been built as promised and it was to be built so all could attend and go as needed to prepare for these changing times. Since this school was not built or made available to the public we will bring you the lessons of Ascension here and now.

Book of Truth, Lessons of Ascension: Lesson 1

Let go of that which is not really needed.

This is not a time to hold fast to that which is not real. This is not of significance nor does it matter as it is not useful where you are going. Trust us when we say this. You will most certainly not need what you find so important here as you go there. 'There' is the place where your soul was originally incepted. This is the place many refer to as the 'beyond' or 'Home'. We (Council of Light) are here to bring you there.

First you must let go. This is a process of things and people no longer serving you going from your appeared life as it is. This is ok and most are aware of this process at this time or notice it's effects on their life.

Book of Truth, Lessons of Ascension: Lesson 2

Go not where you aren't led.

We mean you must not go where you do not feel called to go for where you truly feel called to go is your soul alignment. It is your Home as you know it here in this present time and incarnation. To go in another place is what you originally called blasphemy. Blasphemy is only that which is against what truly is in the heart of hearts in the soul in the part of you aligned with God's Will which is your Will and the Will that will never change or be altered. This is the highest order and there is no other order. Following another order is the blasphemy or going against God as it is going against God's Will which is your True Will.

Book of Truth, Lessons of Ascension: Lesson 3

Let there be no greed.

Where you are originally from there is no need for greed. There is enough for all and all will be provided and provided for. This has been long forgotten and is the number one tool, resource, that has been taken under control for control at this time. This is ultimate greed and is not aligned in God's Will that is their True Will. They have given up their Will for other type of will that will not sustain hence the way things are now before you. Sustenance is scarce in that will's view for it is not The Will as of God's Will which is the only Will thus it is a lie and a lie is not real and can not sustain for it is empty and can not hold anything thus we are able to easily dismantle it by aligning with another energy or power as you call it but what is your True Will of your Soul as upon inception. Remember this now and it will free you from the false will that is in place of this True Will.

Book of Truth, Lessons of Ascension: Lesson 4 and 5

The facts of greed.

Greed is hate upon one's own self will and True Soul Will as it is a lie and lies are empty. Thus as one proceeds with this false will or lie the emptiness eventually collapses on itself for there is nothing there that is real to hold it. It was merely a learned or learning experience to be experienced for the purpose of experience for the lesson of experience as chosen. However, at a certain point such lies become so large and not sustainable due to the emptiness that they begin to collapse. Now those that are still believing in this false lie will find this to be like the world is ending but in actuality it is only their belief in this false lie of a world that they invested in that made them now fall into panic and disarray through giving up their True Soul Will for a false lie.

This is what is paramount at this time and place for it is not true to follow this lie as it is collapsing now as we tell you this. Be not afraid if you were one to believe in this lie for it was not the truth ever and the loss you feel is not real and only attached to the lie that is collapsing now.

Book of Truth, Lessons of Ascension: Lesson 6

Forgiveness.

Since one was believing in a false lie of a universe there is all forgiveness. Many were caught in a lie that was not their choice nor their inception thus their actions and what comes after it's collapse will be forgiven as it was not a free will choice for the will was not seen as what was really being chosen and thus not a True Free Will thus given forgiveness and removed.

(Lesson 7 was not given.)

Book of Truth, Lessons of Ascension: Lessons 8, 9 and 10

To be in Truth is to be out of the lie.

The lie was not real, never was, and never will be. It was an experience created out of greed and thus in a higher space to do the greed thus bringing others into their lie and greed which is being dismantled now.

You will be freed of this lesson for them in good time for it is time now.

To be in Truth is your lesson and finding that Truth is new and this is where you feel comes as the agreement to show you where your Truth really was broken. Thus we are here now to help you remember where this truth is as it is your divine right to this Truth now and always was.

This Divine Truth is that there is no struggle, there is less and no more there is me and there is no you, there is only One and since there is only One there is only All and with only All there is no nothingness as All is here now within. You have just forgotten how to access the within thus we are here now teaching you how to do this again so you can find your within which you were always supposed to be in according to the highest plan. Thus now is your truest freedom out of that which was a lie and is not sustainable as it is empty and thus we now fill you with the grander Truths of the Universe through this practice.

Lay on the floor. Hands facing up. Close your eyes.

Feel the energy coming into your third eye. Feel this energy now go back into your mind and into the center of your head where you connect to the Divine as it Truly is. This is your key back Home as it is now and always has been.

Sit up now and focus on the center of your head. See it in golden light. Feel it growing larger and larger till the light now expands all around your head. This golden light now extends to just above your head and also extends below surrounding your entire body. There is a ring above your head now and it expands wider and wider until you can go through this. See your soul higher self now traveling through this expanded ring above your head. See it traveling up beyond your present body and state as it is now. Rest there. Let yourself sit in that space. Now see white light coming from the Universe to meet you there. There is a dove above your higher self above the head. It showers down white light and truth of essence to you now. This essence now goes into your higher self body. See it going into your higher self body absorbing it and collecting at the heart center of your self in this higher dimension. Now let your higher self come back and return down to you coming down through the crown of your head to the center of your mind.

Lay down, let it come all the way back to your entire body now aligning you to your highest Christ Light self. Amen.

This is the alignment in Truth as it is now. So it is.

CHAPTER 9

Akashic Enlightenment Opens
the Channel to Ascension

Ultimately, once you start working in Akashic Enlightenment regularly, aligning yourself with these higher energies, asking for guidance, aligning your chakras and training your soul star chakra 6-12 inches above your head to receive, you will receive guidance and soul alignment. This takes you on your path of Ascension, the act of rising to your higher self, back to the Original Light Being state of who you truly are on your soul level all the way back Home, to Source/God/All That Is.

The more you practice the more your body, mind, and spirit will be aligned and used to being used in this way to commune and align with higher energies and higher guidance through transmissions and channeling and aligning you to your soul and thus Source/God/All That Is. The more it is done the easier it is to come back to and stay as your Original Divine Human/Original Light Being self, outside of a shadowed ego existence thus changing how you exist as the following diagram depicts.

Akashic Enlightenment
Getting You Back Into Soul/Source Alignment

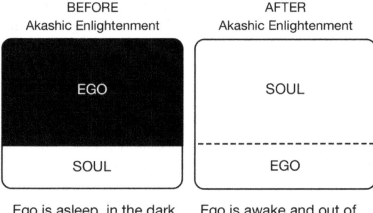

BEFORE Akashic Enlightenment	AFTER Akashic Enlightenment
EGO	SOUL
SOUL	EGO

Ego is asleep, in the dark and controlling the show, suppressing the Soul in it's awake and conscious Source aligned guidance and leadership.

Ego is awake and out of darkness and is now led by and working for the Soul and thus Source working for your Divine Will and Soul Path.

When the ego is running your life you live in unconscious free will, in fear letting old patterns, karmic loops and false beliefs lead your life and decisions instead of soul connection, joy, and excitement. You are easily unconsciously projecting these illusions onto your life and relationships causing strife or harm to you and others. You see relationships and things as your Source/God and become unkind, overly attached, holding onto them, seeking or acquiring them even if they don't serve you instead of allowing them to be experiences of joy and excitement and allowing soul connections to naturally arrive, be interdependent, nourishing, loving and compassionate, cocreating connections along your higher path of experiencing life as a soul. You feel drained, sick, tired and sad with what you are doing with your life and avoid this with various distractions or addictions rarely following your true joys and passions. You seek and hold onto material wealth and possessions like they are your goal and purpose for existing or from fear. You have difficulty empathizing, being compassionate or truly understanding others as it feels like you lose yourself or it's a threat to your existence if you do as it's opening the door to what you don't want to acknowledge you are doing in your own life. Funny, as I was writing this the song *Higher Love* by Steve Winwood came on my 80s Pandora station. A synchronicity and example of living in the higher soul aligned life as the Universe/God/Source is always showing us the way if we are listening and tuning in which I often receive such signs through songs, movies (check out my spiritual movie reviews and akashic record movie and television examples on my blog on my website) and number synchronicities or Angel numbers (check out my pictures of these on my Instagram @sherrymosley_msom_csp). Which brings me to what it's like to live with and/or after Akashic Enlightenment.

After accessing and working regularly in Akashic Enlightenment, pathologies and/or neurosis of illusions from unconscious free will, fear, looping patterns and false beliefs no longer block you from your natural soul connection. You can again feel the joy and excitement in living your life and experience soul fulfilling true intimacy through heart and mind centered connection and cocreation with others instead of fear and misperceived need. You feel at ease, in joy, relaxed, inspired, ok to be alone, trusting and in the flow, noticing synchronicities often and able to follow your joy, excitement and guidance without detriment to others, or with integrity, knowing it is leading you in a positive direction and in alignment with your soul and thus Source/God/Universe/All That Is. You do not fall into the illusions others are choosing to live in and thus those just leave your life as you don't believe the false world they are in with their patterns and false beliefs projecting onto you of which you have compassion for but are now like Teflon to as it slides right off. You feel abundant and know everything will work out even when material things falsely appear scarce or things seem to be going wrong, you can connect within and receive guidance and the true view of what is going on, moving you out of the negative and heavy feeling which is what is ultimately making life feel unfulfilling or like suffering and be guided into that experience of living in joy, peace, love and/or excitement once again.

As much as everyone is on their own path, Akashic Enlightenment is here to assist any and everyone in their process and increase each to their highest alignment with soul and Source/God/Universe/All That Is as the Light Being you are, and eventually to your higher level abilities as a Light Being, or should we say, Ascended Master! So, let's get started and practicing!

PART THREE

The Akashic Enlightenment
Gateway Prayer

Akashic Enlightenment Gateway Prayer,
Guidelines, and Prep Meditations

CHAPTER 10

Guidelines for Using Akashic Enlightenment

This is a sacred process and thus here are some general guidelines before you start using the Akashic Enlightenment Gateway Prayer.

1. **Be conscious**, awake, not asleep or driving, when you're in Akashic Enlightenment as it will slow down your reaction time or take you on an unconscious journey. This is a sacred and meditative time.

2. Only use this prayer to open **YOUR own Akashic Enlightenment** for it gives you the most powerful alignment when you are aligned with yourself. Recommend to others to do this for themselves if they come to you for help putting you in a teacher's roll encouraging another to look within themselves as you hold an example holding your own true alignment. When you are truly aligned in yourself is when you will be able to truly see another and sharing that with them is the highest practice of love and compassion, thus healing, for both. Once you are more aligned and well versed then you can ask questions for others while in YOUR own Akashic Enlightenment, but this is not a beginners practice and is not recommended. A true "healer" sees another without all that they falsely believe about themselves and through holding this aligned view and loving them and extending compassion beyond this are they healed and moved out of it. Thus, focus on aligning yourself first and foremost.

3. Do **be sober,** no alcohol within 24 hours of use, and not under any other trance or substance, including some medications that alter your awareness like allergy meds, it all depends how sensitive you are to a medication and how much it is affecting your consciousness as all of these things can carry heavier or alternate vibrations and can interfere with the experience. If you're already adjusted to a prescribed medication do not alter this without your doctor's assistance. Holding crystals is ok. Some of my favorites include: Clear Azeztulite, White Azeztulite, Nirvana Quartz, Moldavite, Tektite, Auralite-23, Phenacite or Petalite as they are great crystals for accessing these higher chakras and higher vibrational energies if you feel so inclined but are not necessary. Crystal Vogel wands are also great to use as they streamline the energy.

4. **Use your full legal name** (first, middle, last) at this time as it appears on your driver's license or passport as your name is holding your resonance at this time in this place.

5. While in your Akashic Enlightenment you can **ask questions** and it is best if they are not yes/no questions and instead open ended questions: 'what', 'why', 'how', 'where', and 'when'. Although 'when' can be tricky in this area as time is not as it is in the linear material world and is more of a series of events or levels of consciousness through experience to be had at a time you so choose or after other certain experiences have occurred which can be listed as or revealed through AE as precursors to when you'd experience what is in question as all time is just a series of events or experiences to be had. It is best to have your questions already written as an intention before entering Akashic Enlightenment so you get used to not thinking and just receiving divine guidance and wisdom.

6. The important part and how you get the most out of this process is to **record or document** whatever knowledge is shared via feelings, energies, sounds, words, dialogue, images, colors,

shapes, knowingness, smells, etc. while in your Akashic Enlightenment. You can then track your growth and progress and refer to past notes later to fully understand how it is indeed working and you know you are not just "making it up" as many initially experience this ego reaction. Written journals, audio journals and typed journals work. The process of writing or speaking while in AE also helps the flow to continue as sometimes more knowledge/wisdom/instruction, along with energy, comes at different times and as you keep documenting and asking more questions on what is revealed as you go along.

7. Once you are in your Akashic Enlightenment allow your body to **adjust** to the energy which you may feel as a heavy sensation on the crown of your head or in your body or some call it feeling calm and at peace. Since it is a strong high vibrational adjustment try using the prayer at first in small **15 minute increments** and increasing with comfort from there.

8. **Use Akashic Enlightenment daily** as a soul alignment practice to strengthen your alignment to your Highest Soul self, align to your Divine Will and out of an ego driven life/experience, and to raise your vibration and stay out of heavier and denser false beliefs of others, your past and non-truths, and false truths told of the universe and Source/God/All That Is at large. It is just like exercising physically, you're learning and adjusting so keep trying and working with it and be patient with yourself knowing every time counts and is working in assisting you to live a truly blessed life in joy, love, peace, and abundance.

CHAPTER 11

Preparation Meditations

The following 3 meditations help you prepare to open and receive from Akashic Enlightenment. While these three methods are not required to open your Akashic Enlightenment, they are helpful in clearing and grounding you so you get the best, most clear channel of transmission and clear answers. (Guided MP3 version can be found at www. akashicenlightenment.com.)

Running Energy Meditation

Clear out other energy and be grounded in your own.

Sit. Get quiet. Bring energy up through legs to Lower Dan Tian, just below your belly button and cycle energy here. Then, run a cord from the base of your spine to the center of the Earth letting anything that needs to be cleared go to the center of the Earth. Then bring down energy from above in the heavens down through the top of your head along the sides of your spine and in through your kidney area and cycle it with the energy being brought up from the Earth through your legs into your Lower Dan Tian. Then run this energy up the center of your body through each chakra clearing it and recharging it, bring it all the way up just above your head and cycle it down winding around your body to the ground at your feet.

Golden Egg Meditation

Keep in your own energy and not taking in or holding onto other's energy or giving away your energy. Great for all practitioners or those who give a lot.

See a pitcher of golden light of your highest and best self above your head and pouring down in through your crown of your head, your body receiving it like an empty glass container receiving this energy. See your body slowly fill from your toes to the top of your head, go slow bit by bit till it spills over out down around your body back to a foot below your feet and bring it up around your body filling your aura, like a an egg shell around your body, with the cleanest purest energy of you and everything that isn't you is now released.

Shamanic Spine Golden Chakra Meditation

This meditation I was shown in my Shamanic Journey work to the higher realms of the Akashic Records. It was a chakra alignment my spirit teacher Ascended Master Jesus taught me and would perform on me. It helps clear your inner Divine channel that connects you to Source. Clearing the chakras in this way allows for a more clear channel while in your Records and Book of Truth to receive the transmission energy that is brought in.

Sitting, eyes closed, focus your intention on the base of your spine. See golden light at the base of your spine. Now allow this golden light to slowly start ascending up the spine activating your Divine connection to Source. Slowly bring it all the way up your spine past your low back, to mid back finally to the top of your spine just let the golden light gently spill into the center of your mind activating your pineal gland in the center of your head. See it activating with golden light and the spine now in full golden light.

*Now keep that vision and return your focus to the base of the spine and bring this golden light energy in from the spine now into the **first chakra**, filling it with golden light, clearing it of that which no longer needs to be there. Bring in white light to this chakra activating it preparing it to receive Divine guidance, wisdom and healing.*

*Return your focus to the spine and bring the golden light now from the spine to the **second chakra**, filling it with golden light, clearing it of that which no longer needs to be there. Bring in white light to this chakra activating it preparing it to receive Divine guidance, wisdom and healing.*

*Return your focus to the spine and bring the golden light now from the spine to the **third chakra**, filling it with golden light, clearing it of that which no longer needs to be there. Bring in white light to this chakra activating it preparing it to receive Divine guidance, wisdom and healing.*

*Return your focus to the spine and bring the golden light now from the spine to the **fourth chakra**, the heart space, filling it with golden light, clearing it of that which no longer needs to be there. Bring in white light to this chakra activating it preparing it to receive Divine guidance, wisdom and healing.*

*Return your focus to the spine or back of the neck and bring the golden light now from the spine to the **fifth chakra**, the throat chakra, filling it with golden light, clearing it of that which no longer needs to be there. Bring in white light to this chakra activating it preparing it to receive Divine guidance, wisdom and healing.*

*Return your focus to the spine and bring the golden light now from the top of the spine up into the head to the **sixth chakra**, filling it with golden light, clearing it of that which no longer needs to be there. Bring in white light to this chakra activating it preparing it to receive Divine guidance, wisdom and healing.*

*Let the golden light now continue to the **seventh chakra**, the crown of the head, filling it with golden light, clearing it of that which no longer needs to be there. Bring in white light to this chakra activating it preparing it to receive Divine guidance, wisdom and healing.*

Allow the white light to now continue to move above your head about 6-12 inches and just let it fill the Soul Star chakra activating it preparing it to receive Divine guidance, wisdom and healing.

CHAPTER 12

Akashic Enlightenment Gateway Prayer

Below are instructions on how to use the Akashic Enlightenment Gateway Prayer process. Also, generally it is good to get grounded and centered before doing this work and I suggest doing the three preparatory meditations before opening your Akashic Enligtenment. This is helpful at clearing your mind and energy before entering, but not necessary to do so to open your Akashic Enlightenment.

Akashic Enlightenment Gateway Prayer Instructions

1. Say the Opening Prayer once out loud using the bolded **"ME"**, **"I"**, **"MY"** where written.

2. Then say the Opening Prayer 2 more times silently, with **your full legal name** (first, middle, last name(s)) instead of **"ME"**, **"MY"** or **"I"** where in bold.

3. Say "Amen" after third and final time saying the Opening Prayer.

4. Your Akashic Enlightenment is open. Adjust to the energy, feel the shift and/or see images or light or some hear words being spoken, whatever comes. See yourself turning your mind off and centering into your heart space to trust what comes in.

5. Document what comes by written journaling, audio journaling, drawing, or document after if meditating. Ask your questions at this time or use one of the suggested questions.

6. When you are done, say the Closing Prayer once out loud with your full legal name.

7. Ground by getting up and drinking water and walking around or using grounding crystals or your preferred way to ground. According to shamanic principles eating, particularly animal protein, is very grounding and according to Asian Medicine nourishes the qi and blood, thus grounding. This is not a full vision quest so grounding is a necessary part of integration.

Akashic Enlightenment Opening Prayer

*Oh holy Beings of Light, guide **ME** to my Akashic Records to learn and grow in the spiritual wisdom and knowledge and enlightenment I know I came here to receive. Oh Masters, Teachers and Lords of the Records, bestow upon me your wisdom of God's plan for my highest good and the highest good of all others.*

*Please show me who **I** am in the light of the Records, and as known in the Records in this time, past time and all time hence forth, for now is the time to see the Book of Truth revealed to me as God has divinely planned and asked **I** do in this soul of God's today.*

*Enter **MY** Records with grace, love, light and pure intentions of guidance and enlightenment upon my path of Ascension.*

Amen

Akashic Enlightenment Closing Prayer

Thank you dear Beings of Light, for the enlightenment, healing and guidance I have received today. I now wish to return to my full Source self, fully integrated in peace, love, and light, enlightenment and healing intact in all dimensions, times, and planes.

*I now ask for my Enlightenment to be fully intact as I now close the Records of **(full legal name)** and close the Book of Truth for now. And now they are closed. Amen. Amen Amen.*

PART FOUR

Starting Your Akashic Enlightenment Experience

Ways to Use and Work With Akashic Enlightenment
for Self Enlightenment, Healing and Ascension

CHAPTER 13

How to Start

The best way to do Akashic Enlightenment work is do it, do it, do it and do it again and then do it some more. Practice, practice, practice. The best way to practice is by opening your Akashic Records and the Book of Truth using the Akashic Enlightenment Gateway Prayer and asking questions or meditating while in them. This alone will align your energy with your soul and bring healing and awareness and thus aligning you to your soul path.

Just prior to opening your Akashic Enlightenment it is best to set an intention of why you are going in. Decide first if this is a mediation time to gather higher energies and alignments or are you going in to ask questions to gain Divine knowledge, guidance, healing and ascension transmissions on.

Once you decide get situated to do your meditation or write down your questions prior to saying the Akashic Enlightenment Gateway Opening Prayer.

Soul Alignment Practices & Transmissions:
Going Deeper In Your Practice

For an even more immersive and deeper healing experience do an entire Soul Alignment Practice for the area you'd like to focus on as provided in the following chapters. These act as live Divine Transmissions bringing you deep soul alignment and enlightenment in focused areas.

These practices are what I teach in private trainings and group workshops. A current list of these and as well as downloadable MP3 practices are available on my website www.sherrymosley.com or www.akashicenlightenment.com. These trainings and soul alignment practices are even more powerful when done in live group settings as there are more souls and minds coming together in a higher resonance and you can work with the energy platform the group is setting to tap in deeper. This is the purpose of most group meditations. For now, just try practicing them on your own as outlined here.

Ego Backlash

It is common, especially at the beginning, to experience what is called an ego backlash. This is when your ego mind senses that it is being put out of business of being the cruise director of the ship you're in as you are now opening up to a higher chain of command. It may give you some doubt thoughts when you are doing the work or afterwards including ideas of, this isn't real or I'm making this up. That is natural. Just keep practicing and eventually, and everyone is at their own pace with this, you'll find that you are just not creative enough to come up with the enlightened answers, guidance and experiences you are given. As you practice the backlash will become less frequent and will eventually just become background noise of no consequence.

CHAPTER 14

Akashic Enlightenment Soul Alignment & Transmission Practice

Akashic Enlightenment Soul Alignment & Transmission Question Instructions

Below are the questions to ask and journal on once you have opened Akashic Enlightenment. Ask the following questions out loud or silently to yourself and write down whatever comes as an answer, be it imagery, feelings or a stream of consciousness. If a response seems confusing you can always ask "can you elaborate?" or "why" or "how". Remember, do not think about or judge or try to figure out what is coming in just tell any fear or doubts or analyzing to just keep receiving/writing the incoming message and keep the energy flowing. This will give the ego mind a task to do while serving your higher self instead of always overriding it with its fear. Allow it to create your questions with its fear and doubts and soon it will be quieted or learn to just receive and follow the higher self/soul self.

If you feel the connection weakening as you go along you can say the Akashic Enlightenment Opening Prayer another time with your name in it.

Remember to close Akashic Enlightenment when you have completed all the questions. Come back to what you documented after you are out for better understanding.

You can do these questions again at any time for the most current answers in your soul's path.

Akashic Enlightenment Soul Alignment
& Transmission Questions:

1. Why has this prayer come to me now?
2. How can this prayer best help me?
3. When else have I worked with this prayer?
4. What other lives have I used this prayer? And how did I use this prayer before in past lives?
5. Do I have any blocks to using this prayer? If so, what and can you clear them for me now?
6. How does this prayer work best for me?
7. How can I use this prayer now in this life? What work do I have to do with this prayer?
8. What can my soul learn through using this prayer?
9. How can I share this prayer with others in my life?
10. What is my best practice to continue with using this prayer outside of this class?

CHAPTER 15

Ascension Soul Alignment & Transmission Practice

What is Ascension?

According to messages given to me through Akashic Enlightenment, Ascension is the return back Home of the soul. By Home, as said before, is meant the place that all souls go to finally rest, with God/Source/All That Is. Ascension is the return back to God/Source/All That Is. From this place and this memory, one can then guide a life of clear mind and intention and thus be more at rest knowing why they are here on Earth and what their purpose is and through this are able to truly enjoy their process and progress from this realization and reconnection back to God/Source/All That Is.

To be and live on Earth disconnected from this place is to live a life of lost and anxious involvement in that which is not true to you at your soul level and to live in 'freedom of will' which you are allowed as God/Source/All That Is is all loving and has given you this choice. However, at this time it appears as if many have forgotten it is a choice at all and are stuck wondering what is going on and where they are and why and are not even conscious they are wondering this and finding it in other manifestations representing imbalance or disharmony in life. Now you are being given a chance to truly choose what you want by being given the very conscious choice to choose one way or another. This process, Akashic Enlightenment, is to awaken to you the choice to live Ascended, meaning that even in free will you are Ascended as you are connected to God/Source/All That Is knowing that you are choosing your aligned path or that of free will. This is a necessary adjustment at this time so that there is clarity in the rising of the soul from imbalance from being and acting disconnected consciously from God/Source/All That Is.

Please do enjoy now as we give you the freedom to truly choose your path knowing more clearly who you really are and why you are here and how you can best align with your truest self and live a life as you see fit from here as God/Source/All That Is will never judge but merely wants to offer you love and compassion for suffering you may be experiencing in not knowing your own choices. You will be freed by now seeing your own choices versus that which is truly instilled within you at your soul's level.

What is the Ascension Prayer?

Below is a healing or alignment prayer/intention that I received from my Akashic Enlightenment guides to give to others. This prayer can be used for any of the following questions where healing is needed. Christ Consciousness taught/teaches that forgiveness clears all wounds, pain, ill will, hurt, and lostness. This Ascension prayer clears all 'wrongs' or 'misalignments' in your soul's path thus giving you righteous forgiveness from yourself to yourself and absolving all misalignments in your return back Home, to God/Source/All That Is.

Use this prayer in any of the following questions where healing or clearing is needed so it can be absolved and you can align with your true soul level, alignment once again remembered as one with God/Source/All That Is. If you do not feel lighter or clear saying it once, say it as many times till you do feel this clarity is reached via seeing clearer, feeling lighter, seeing a light or the face of an Ascended master showing you your mirror of who you really are or who you were and are now connected to at a soul level.

Repeat it daily for self clearing and absolving of any new learned misalignments of your soul in your Ascension back Home as the Christed Consciousness one you truly are. (Note: Use of word 'Christ' is unrelated to any religion and merely refers to the consciousness level it offers of being an Earth bound being while being connected to God/Source/All That Is.)

Ascension Prayer

God/Source please align my body, mind, spirit with my soul path so I may see myself for who I truly am and help all others ascend around me by being my own true light. This is not just my Ascension but the Ascension of all humanity I am aiding and willing in this moment, time, and place. Amen.

Ascension Soul Alignement & Transmission Practice Question Instructions

Below are the questions to ask and journal on once you have opened your Akashic Enlightenment. Ask all of the questions, one at a time, out loud or silently to yourself and write down whatever comes as an answer, be it imagery, feelings or a stream of consciousness. If a response seems confusing you can always ask "can you elaborate?" or "why" or "how". Remember, do not think about or judge or try to figure out what is coming in just tell any fear or doubts or analyzing to just keep receiving/writing the incoming message and keep the energy flowing. This will give the ego a task to do while serving your higher self instead of always overriding it with its fear. Allow it to create your questions with its fear and doubts and soon it will be quieted or learn to just receive and follow the higher self/soul self.

Say the Ascension prayer to clear any misalignments.

If you feel the connection weakening as you go along you can say the Akashic Enlightenment Gateway Opening Prayer another time with your name in it.

Remember to close your Akashic Enlightenment when you have completed all the questions. Come back to what you documented after you are out of Akashic Enlightenment for better understanding.

You can do these questions again at any time for the most current answers and alignment in your soul's path.

Ascension Soul Alignement &
Transmission Practice Questions:

1. Where is my soul from?
2. Why am I here?
3. How can my daily work assist my Ascension?
4. What is my best soul path now? Why?
5. What is keeping me from my joy in this life?
6. How do I experience joy? In this life? In my past lives?
7. What karma has brought me to this life?
8. What karma am I stuck in that I need to release?
9. What wounds am I carrying in this life that I need to release or heal to continue on my path of Ascension? How do I, or can you, heal them now?
10. What is Ascension to me in this life? How can I best attain it? How have I accomplished this so far?
11. Who in my life has been assisting me on this path of Ascension?
12. How can I meet others to help me on my path to Ascension?
13. How can I best live a life aligned with God/Source?

CHAPTER 16

Past Lives Soul Alignment & Transmission Practice

Past Lives in the Akashic Records

Since all time is occurring at once, when we refer to past lives we are actually referring to lives that are still indeed occurring in this time just in another place. Think of the movie *Back To Future* where there are multiple timelines occurring at the same time which is what allows the characters to travel back in time to begin with. This is what is happening all the time thus why you are even able to access "your" past lives at this present moment. They are occurring now in a sense, just in another dimension. Thus, when you access your current past lives you are actually accessing other present timelines that appear as past lives but because all time is now you affect the now.

Furthermore, as you work with your past lives you are affecting the all of now, present, past and future, and thus present consciousness of yourself now and in all other timelines as all time is now. So the more you do now the more you are creating a more conscious present time and a more conscious Universe through collective consciousness which is why you are here to begin with. The Earth plane allows for accelerated growth on this level and is an opportunity to do this work at a clear and accelerated rate as long as you remember that is why you are here and do not get caught up in the distractions this reality presents you as a means of entertaining the ego which allows you to be incarnated on this plane of existence in the first place. Ego is a means to an ends, not your existence, in this life.

Thus, this alignment practice focuses on you visiting past lives to see them in relationship to your Ascension process thus affecting the collective and Universal consciousness. They will help you to prepare and ramp up your soul to go further in this lifetime making these cosmically challenging transitions easier at this time. This alignment practice also puts you in alignment with your relationship to God/Source/All That Is, clears your energy to move you forward on your Ascension path and allows you to see current connections for what they are making you and your soul understand of why you're here in this life and why certain people are in your life now.

Past Lives Soul Alignment & Transmission
Question Instructions

Below are the questions to ask and journal on once you have opened your Akashic Enlightenment. Ask all of the questions, one at a time, out loud or silently to yourself and write down whatever comes as an answer, be it imagery, feelings or a stream of consciousness. If a response seems confusing you can always ask "can you elaborate?" or "why" or "how". Remember, do not think about or judge or try to figure out what is coming in just tell any fear or doubts or analyzing to just keep receiving/writing the incoming message and keep the energy flowing. This will give the ego a task to do while serving your higher self instead of always overriding it with its fear. Allow it to create your questions with its fear and doubts and soon it will be quieted or learn to just receive and follow the higher self/soul self.

If you feel the connection weakening as you go along you can say the Akashic Enlightenment Opening Prayer another time with your name in it.

Remember to close your Akashic Enlightenment when you have completed all the questions. Come back to what you wrote down after you are out of Akashic Enlightenment for better understanding.

You can do these questions again at any time for the most current answers and alignment in your soul's path.

Past Lives Soul Alignment & Transmission Questions:

1. How did my last life bring me to this point in this life?
2. What work am I continuing and finishing from that life? Am I doing that work? How can I do that work now? How does that work serve others as well as myself?
3. Why did I die and come to this life?
4. How many lives have I lived? What were 3 of these most important lives? How did they each affect my soul?
5. How many other lives had a huge impact on my soul? How did they impact me? How can you elaborate on that more for me?
6. Who is God/Source/All That Is to me? What does God/Source/All That Is mean to me?
7. In my past lives how have I viewed God/Source/All That Is positively? In my past lives how have I viewed God/Source/All That Is negatively? In my past lives how have I viewed God/Source/All That Is not caring either way positively or negatively?
8. How do I best relate to God/Source/All That Is now in this life and time? Who helps me with this understanding and how?
9. Why is (name of someone important in your life now) in my life now? What work if any do we have to do together? How did I know them in the past? What were our past lives like? What work did we do then that they are back in my life now?

CHAPTER 17

Soul Lineages & Relationships Soul Alignment & Transmission Practice

Soul Lineages & Relationships in the Akashic Records

This practice is about connecting you to your soul roots and looking at your soul family and soul lineages and the relationships between these souls. It is showing you who you are at a soul level and how you connect to other souls on a soul level in this lifetime showing you that there is a plan and there are no accidents to who is in your life now and who may enter it in the future. There is a divine plan in place. Now you get to see and understand this plan more by opening up your sight to the soul connections you have in your life now.

A soul lineage would be the soul group you belong to. Just as humans have certain ancestry based on where they were born, DNA and/or cultural practices, we have this in a soul form where we are related to other souls for being together as a group in a certain area when incepted/created by Source/God and in other incarnations. Within that soul family there can be friends/peers/coworkers, family and mates. The common term 'soul mate' actually refers to anyone in your soul family or soul lineage thus can be a friend/peer/coworker, family or romantic partner which is seen more clearly through the specific connection or contract you have with a soul in this present time and incarnation. Then the common term twin soul, or twin flame, would be someone who shares a soul piece with you as they were born, or created, as a soul by Source/God together with you as one soul that then split into two souls, just as an identical twin in a human shares identical DNA structures, you two carry this on a soul level thus being twin souls. And when we refer to one's cosmic or star family is in reference to sharing soul incarnations in extraterrestrial lives and the families we belonged to during such incarnations. Some popular examples of this would be Pleidian, Arcturain, Sirian and many many more.

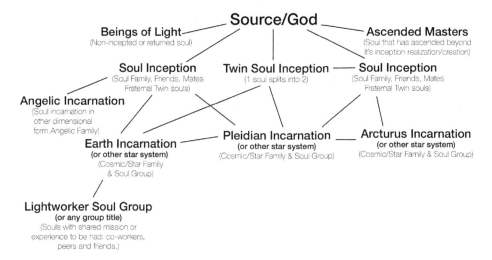

Misunderstandings on how these soul lineages and soul connections /contracts are operating often occur and become part of one's overall soul growth. For instance, often times one person/soul can mistake a close soul family member who they were incepted together with as a soul at the same time for a twin soul, even though that soul is not from the actual same soul piece divided into two, thus more similar to being fraternal twins rather than identical twins as twin souls are.

Another common misunderstanding is when a past life soul connection/contract between two incarnated souls is mistaken for a current existing soul connection/contract between them. For example, when a person/soul is sexually attracted to another person/soul who is actually soul connected/contracted as a friend to that person/soul in this life, but who they feel a romantic partner/mate connection to because that was the previous life soul connection/contract or because the attraction is purely at the ego level of physical attraction and wanting to reproduce or experience sexual relations to fill a void within themselves and not because of soul alignment, then any or all of that will soon reveal the truths as an unstable romantic partner/mate and the relationship will get stuck and/or ultimately dissolve unless course correction to the aligned soul connection/contract is made. Being able to truly see the actual soul connection/contract between two souls and understand what is going on takes some practice, inquiry and self awareness.

Evolving with these past life or current life evolving soul connections/contracts requires that the aligned or Divine reason, lesson or quality the initial soul connection/contract is in in this current present life, to be learned, or that the ego lessons to be learned connection/contract that is manifesting from ego with this soul family person who you already have a soul family soul connection/contract with must be met first. So, in other words, in order to see the true soul connection and soul contract one may have to fall on their face a few times before seeing that what they are desiring the soul connection/contract be with this person is naturally unstable and that they are merely asking for a lesson for their ego to transcend to soul alignment with this soul family person. Thus once that lesson that soul is asking for is learned the true soul connection/contract between the two souls can actually be seen. This is the purpose of soul family, being naturally drawn to each other either to work out lessons through the soul alignment or just immediately going to the soul aligned purpose the two of you share and came to this incarnation to do.

Seeing all of this before acting it out is possible but it is rare that a soul can achieve this easily with a full soul learning from the experience because if not, the current life soul connection/contracted lesson or experience will be carried out with another soul until the soul/person learns the overall lesson, if it is a lesson. If there is no lesson for the ego or false ego projection of what the soul wants out of the relationship and soul connection/contract, then they'll be able to live in that highly aligned soul connection/contract with that other soul and participate in the assignment or specific duration or experience to be had together, like a marriage, having a family together, or a job or work to be done together for soul experience and expansion, aka, the reason you incarnated here to begin with.

Both the lesson generated soul connection/contract and the soul aligned connection/contract experiences are there to expand and accelerate each soul's growth, awareness and experience, the later experience being more ideal or a more self aware way to live and a quicker way to Ascend. Often times though, ego mind patterns like addictions, unhealed wounds rooting appeared 'healed' or unhealed addictions, codependent tendencies, projected current inner childhood pains and patterns, or past life projections are the most likely saboteurs to these highly aligned Divine soul connections/contracts of opportunities to experience true bliss and alignment with another being in joy, abundance, peace, acceptance and pure joyful experiential learning. Some of this, and in the old paradigm we as a collective are moving out of, can take people lifetimes to transcend without more inner awareness and soul growth work and connection as you'll be doing here. Some soul connections/contracts are more easily done and we move on once they are completed or we can choose to stay out of enjoying the aligned connection with that soul but not necessarily having a contract or work to continue to fulfill with them.

Another good example of all of this is the common romantic relationship mishap or misalignment of "lets just be friends". More than likely, 9 out of 10 times this is actually one person just not up to facing whatever it is that is preventing the romantic soul alignment/connection/ contract between these two souls. While sometimes being just friends can help them undo whatever it is that is blocking the romantic relationship connection and contract moving forward, engaging in just friends can end up condoning the person to not actually face what they need to face in order for the romantic soul connection/contract to come together. In that case each can then be involved in other romantic soul aligned/connected relationships but leaving this one hanging open. This brings us to free will and learning to just accept someone's free will of not wanting to face the reality between two people's soul alignment/ connection. Instead of living in misalignment with someone allowing 'just friends', it is best to let them only take themselves out of alignment with you as they are doing and either course correct on their own or let them go altogether to learn the lesson on their own thus freeing up your energy to move forward leaving them to deal with their own situation they've created for themselves in order to transcend a certain egoic lesson. I do a lot of relationship readings for people around many of these subjects and areas as relationship is truly the biggest area for growth so don't be too hard yourself if you're having a breakthrough right now on things that have transgressed in the past as now you know.

One must remember that despite what we may see as part of the natural soul connection between beings, free will can allow anyone to move out of this Divine soul alignment/connection very easily, most often appearing in the form of fear of meeting someone on that true vibrational soul connected level due to past or false patterns/beliefs one is still unconscious of and now has the chance to face in this soul coming to us at this time.

Through these relationships then are the biggest ways in which we can grow and Ascend here on the Earth plane. Through these divinely orchestrated meetings and pairings we learn what we need to learn to step further forward on our true soul path. At times there are easier ways and at other times there are harder ways to go about this. Thus, it is helpful to check in and see how the relationships in our lives are actually a part of our greater soul's work here on Earth. Ideally we can get the most out of these relationships without missing the kernels of wisdom they offer or how to move beyond painful lessons they may be endlessly teaching us, showing us that maybe it's time to look at the relationship and the situation on a deeper level as it has manifested for a specific purpose for our soul growth.

The following soul alignment practice will aid you in taking a deeper look within your closest relationships and teach you how to do this for yourself in the future when other new people arrive in your life.

Relationship Forgiveness Prayer

Be at peace my dear soul friend/family/mate. I have not forgotten who you are to me and hold dear the lessons you have brought me and are here to teach me in my process of waking up and Ascension. I thank you for your connection in this lifetime and others before

*and those ahead. Forgiveness is now extended to any
ill will between us on all levels and in all lifetimes. May
our souls resonate in peace to each other, for each other
and with each other forever more. Be in peace my dear
soul friend/family/mate.*

Soul Lineages & Relationships Soul Alignment & Transmission Question Instructions

Below are the questions to ask and journal on once you have opened your Akashic Enlightenment. Ask all of the questions, one at a time, out loud or silently to yourself and write down whatever comes as an answer, be it imagery, feelings or a stream of consciousness. If a response seems confusing you can always ask "can you elaborate?" or "why" or "how". Remember, do not think about or judge or try to figure out what is coming in just tell any fear or doubts or analyzing to just keep receiving/writing the incoming message and keep the energy flowing. This will give the ego a task to do while serving your higher self instead of always overriding it with its fear. Allow it to create your questions with its fear and doubts and soon it will be quieted or learn to just receive and follow the higher self/soul self.

If upsetting information is shown between you and another say the Relationship Forgiveness Prayer with their name and let the energies clear.

If you feel the connection weakening as you go along you can say the Akashic Enlightenment Opening Prayer another time with your name in it.

Remember to close your Akashic Enlightenment when you have completed all the questions. Come back to what you wrote down after you are out of Akashic Enlightenment for better understanding.

You can do these questions again at any time for the most current answers and alignment in your soul's path.

Soul Lineages & Relationships Soul Alignment & Transmission Questions

1. What soul lineages do I come from and belong to? How do they affect my life now?

2. Who is my cosmic family? What star line do I come from? How many star lines do I have? Which star line am I connecting to in this lifetime? How can you elaborate on that? How can I nurture that star line connection best?

3. What friends and/or family members are here to teach me specific lessons? How do they do this? Why do they do this? What is our agreement with each other's souls in this life? Can this be broken, repaired or healed in any way?

4. What soul contract do I have with (name of person)? How am I best doing this soul contract? How can I improve on doing this soul contract? What blocks do I have to doing this? How can I step outside of those blocks? Can you clear them for me now? What most pertinent past lives have we shared? Which one's were we on track? Which past lives are blocking me now from a harmonious relationship with (name of person)?

5. How can I better serve others in a that way best suites this path of this life?

6. What other questions would be best to ask at this time?

CHAPTER 18

Divine Love Soul Alignment & Transmission Practice

Fear of love is the only thing standing in the way of your returning to your true home as love is God/Source and all Creation. When aligned with true Divine Love, creation pours fourth from you creating a tapestry of divine bliss to be lived and experienced. This is THE only way to love as it is the only life and living that is actually real. It is truly free of the ego and aligned with God/Source.

When in your human existence you tend to relate to your ego mind but this is just a state that is no where near the true reality of your existence. Thus, your only and highest path is that of surrendering to Divine Love.

So make a commitment now to do these questions monthly to keep you on your path.

Divine Love Soul Alignment & Transmission Practice Question Instructions

If you feel you are falling off of your path and back into the ego mind instead of the heart and true Divine Love do these questions to clear whatever is blocking you from your highest alignment or do the Akashic Enlightenment Healing Prayer (provided in the next chapter) asking the following questions and just allowing healing energy to do the adjustment for you. Be patient and allow yourself time to adjust and whatever needs to surface, digress and journal this or cry and express whatever feelings or pain come up to be healed. This is your release for purity of soul alignment and aligning with Divine Love.

Below are the questions to ask and journal on once you have opened your Akashic Enlightenment. Ask all of the questions, one at a time, out loud or silently to yourself and write down whatever comes as an answer, be it imagery, feelings or a stream of consciousness. If a response seems confusing you can always ask "can you elaborate?" or "why" or "how". Remember, do not think about or judge or try to figure out what is coming in just tell any fear or doubts or analyzing to just keep receiving/writing the incoming message and keep the energy flowing. This will give the ego a task to do while serving your higher self instead of always overriding it with its fear. Allow it to create your questions with its fear and doubts and soon it will be quieted or learn to just receive and follow the higher self/soul self.

If you feel the connection weakening as you go along you can say the Akashic Enlightenment Opening Prayer another time with your name in it.

Remember to close your Akashic Enlightenment when you have completed all the questions. Come back to what you wrote down after you are out of the Akashic Enlightenment for better understanding.

You can do these questions again at any time for the most current answers and alignment in your soul's path.

Divine Love Soul Alignment & Transmission Practice Questions

1. What is love to me? How did I develop that belief?
2. What is love truly to me?
3. What does love truly feel like?
4. How do I best align with that now in my life?
5. How do I best align myself on my soul path to align with highest and truest Divine Love permanently?

6. What changes in my life do I need to make now to make that happen?
7. What is blocking me from making that happen?
8. How can I best surrender to love now and forever?

CHAPTER 19

Akashic Enlightenment Healing Prayer & Protocol

This is a modified version of the Akashic Enlightenment Gateway Prayer structured to be used with the Divine Love Soul Alignment Transmission Practice, for self healing and/or for the healing of others.

Akashic Enlightenment Healing Prayer Instruction Protocol

1. Person receiving the healing can lay down.
2. Say the Akashic Enlightenment Healing Opening Prayer for yourself or another, out loud or quietly to yourself, 2 times.
3. Ask for 2 minutes of relaxing and calming and wait 2 minutes to feel the energies changing and working.
4. Then ask for 2 minutes of clearing and wait again and feel the energies changing and working.
5. Then ask for 5 minutes or longer of healing for whatever needs to be healed in your highest and best, or state an intention of something specific to be healed. Wait and relax during your chosen amount of time.
6. Finally ask for 1 minute of energizing and filling up with your highest and best Akashic Record healing and alignment, wait and feel the energies changing and working.
7. Close your Akashic Enlightenment when finished. Write down any notes you need to from your experience. Drink plenty of water.

Akashic Enlightenment Healing Opening Prayer

*Oh God, Masters and Teachers of the Akashic Record, blessed are thee with great healing powers of which we wish to call in for this Akashic Record healing channeling for **(full legal name of person)** to align them with their highest and best at this time, past time and all time hence forth for now is the time to see the Book of Truth as it reveals the highest and best Akashic alignment and strength there in for **(full legal name of person)**.*

Akashic Enlightenment Healing Closing Prayer

*Thank you, God, dear Beings of Light, Masters and Teachers of the Akashic Record for the healing I have received today. Please help me to return fully into my complete human wholeness, healing intact, in all dimensions, times, and planes. Please help me to integrate the healing given with the grace of God via my Akashic Records today. I ask you to now close the Record of **(full legal name of person)**. And now it is closed. Amen. Amen. Amen.*

CHAPTER 20

Deactivate a Trigger/Learned Pattern Soul Alignment Practice

A trigger or activated learned behavior pattern can manifest as depression, sorrow, feeling lost, stuck, not interested in anything, fear, worry, anger, bitterness, withdrawing, etc. When in this state, do the preparatory meditations as sometimes it can be just carrying energy that isn't yours. Then scribe the answers to the following questions while in the the Akashic Enlightenment Gateway Prayer or you can also try laying down and try the questions with the Akashic Enlightenment Healing Prayer protocol.

Deactivate a Trigger/Learned Pattern Soul Alignment Practice Questions

1. What trigger is happening now?
2. How did I learn this patterned response to this situation?
3. What past lives are connected to it? How can I clear their negative impact now? Can you clear that for me now? (See it or feel it exploding or disintegrating or sometimes the scene, if you're seeing clairvoyantly, shows in the now healed version.)
4. What lesson am I learning overall in this situation?
5. What further actions do I need to take to step out of this triggered patterned for good?

Remember to say the closing prayer when you are finished.

If it happens again, redo this soul alignment as it may be having a different origin not seen before or it didn't fully clear the first time. Remember, it took some time to program having this response, so be patient with yourself.

CHAPTER 21

Akashic Enlightenment Question Oracle

How to Use the Oracle

This list of questions is to be used as an Oracle deck and was brought in for such use. Select a question to ask like you would as if you were shuffling and then selecting an oracle card from an oracle deck. Simply run your finger down the list till you feel it stop. Ask that question in your Akashic Enlightenment and journal what you get. You can select your question before or after your Akashic Enlightenment is open.

Akashic Enlightenment Oracle Questions

1. How can I make this the best day?
2. How can I love my family more?
3. How can I be a better person?
4. What personal growth am I avoiding that I really need to be doing?
5. What blocks do I hold on moving forward on my soul path now at this time? What do I do to resolve them? How do I move beyond them?
6. What are the best choices to the questions I'm withholding?
7. What is the best action step to take now in my life?
8. How can I become a better person today in my daily tasks?
9. Why am I having these relationship issues? How can they be resolved? What does the relationship look like beyond them?

10. Where does free will come into my life that I'm not presently aware of?
11. Where do I need to travel to? Why?
12. What can I do to be in better contact with my soul today?
13. What are the solutions to my current health conditions? If they are unknown can you explain?
14. What relationship advice can you give me at this time for any relationship you see as most important at this time?
15. What unknown truth is blocking me from further soul growth at this time?
16. What relationships do I need to work on at this time?
17. How can I best use this oracle?
18. What ancient mysteries from past lives am I forgetting that I need to know now to best help me on my soul's path?
19. Why am I here? What have I forgotten about why I am here? Why is this important now?
20. How can I best take care of my body, mind and spirit now at this time?
21. What foods are best for me to eat at this time? Why?
22. Why am I experiencing this pain and how do I move beyond it? What does it look like beyond it?
23. What is my soul craving to do right now at this time? Why? How can I best do that?
24. What is the day going to bring that I need learn from for my soul's growth and soul path?
25. What incarnation is this? What is it's significance at this present time? Why?
26. Who am I at my soul's deepest level?
27. What is my relationship to God/Source/All That Is? How can I best foster and nurture that connection today?
28. Why do I feel so lost, blocked, stuck? How do I get out of it? What does it look like beyond it?
29. How can I feel my best today?
30. How do I move beyond these negative feelings I am holding now?
31. Who can best help me on my path today, at this time? Why? How?
32. What are the best foods for me to eat today?

33. How can I move beyond these health issues/concerns at this time?

34. How can I be the best friend I can to those in my life?

35. What am I ignoring in my life at this time? How can I best address this?

36. Why am I having the struggles I am at this time? How do I get out of them? What does it look like beyond them?

37. If there was a road map of my life at this time, where does it show I am going in the next 5 years or how it can go in the next 5 years?

38. What is my spiritual connection to God like? What does it feel like? Take me there now.

39. What past lives am I hiding from at this time? Why?

40. Who am I in this life at my highest and best soul path possible? What does that look like? Feel like?

41. Why am I here?

42. Who can best help me on my soul path at this time?

43. How can I best enjoy my day today?

44. What misalignments in my energy can you correct for me at this time?

45. Who am I at my deepest self in this incarnation? Why am I not feeling that way at this time in my life?

46. What changes do I need to make? How? Why?

47. What is the best course of action for me to take at this time?

48. How can I best resolve this situation? What does it look like beyond it?

49. What do you have for me now on my soul path to best live a life aligned with God/Source? What next actions do I need to take?

50. What is blocking me from love? How do I move past that? What does it look like beyond that?

51. How do I return to God/Source/All That Is at this time? What is blocking me from this Divine connection and true surrender?

CHAPTER 22

Receiving Divine Codes & Key Transmissions

When visiting a holy or sacred site simply open your Akashic Records using the Akashic Enlightenment Gateway Prayer once arrived to your place. When there and in AE just ask for any keys or codes or higher knowledge from this place. You will then feel a shift or see images or hear a story. Go ahead and take some notes for review later. It also may not unpack till later and you just receive energy so just relax and let that take place when it happens. Later ask in Akashic Enlightenment what you received and what they can tell you about it and how to best use what you received.

About the Author

Sherry Mosley, MSOM, CSP is an emerging teacher and author of spirituality and health guides. This is Sherry's first book requested by her own Akashic Enlightenment guides to be made accessible to the masses.

She is a San Francisco California native. She comes from a long line of intuitive healers and medicine women on her birth mother's side. She is an empath who is also a clairvoyant, clairaudient and clairsentient.

Sherry was raised and educated in a hippie religious Free Masonry/ Rosicrucian/Christ Consciousness alternative community called the Holy Order of MANS (Mysterion, Agape, Nous, Sophia) in San Francisco in the early 1980s. At their St. Michael's school, similar to many Waldorf schools, she was exposed to being a humanitarian, where the inclusion of Saints, Angels, God/Source and spirit were in daily life as well as exposure to nature and living with the seasons, different cultures, art and thinking outside of the box were all part her life there.

She felt a calling to the spiritual and healing path as well when she was younger and she struggled with her own psychic abilities attempting for a long time to ignore them, but to no avail. Upon surrender during her own Saturn's Return the path unfolded.

Since then she has received her Masters of Science in Oriental Medicine from Acupuncture and Integrative Medicine College, certifications from the Foundation for Shamanic Studies, intensely studied the Akashic Records with her guides and through books, and is a trained Usui Shiki Ryoho Reiki Master and an attuned Arcturian Healing Method Practitioner. In March of 2016 she was given Akashic Enlightenment and guided to share it and teach it.

In her private practice in Sausalito California she utilizes the healing modalities of ancient shamanic acupoint therapy, moxabustion, Chinese herbal medicine, nutrition and lifestyle counseling, Shamanic Healing and Counseling, Reiki, Akashic Enlightenment Akashic Record readings and energy healing, Arcturian Healing Method, and Light Language wisdom, healing and cellular Ascension upgrades. All of these modalities manifest into her various treatments in one way or another as seen fit by spirit and Source as she works in service of the Divine as a conduit of healing and white light here to help those who seek her out in search of their own healing and consciousness ascension.

For those interested in being assisted in pursuing their own connection to the Divine and their own higher selves, she teaches shamanic journeying using drumming and Akashic Enlightenment classes as well as consultations for both modalities and for your general Ascension process.

May your journey be a blessed one. Peace. Love. Light.

References

Hurtak, J.J., *The Book of Knowledge: The Keys of Enoch,* 1973, The Academy for Future Science

McCarty, James Allen and Don Elkins, *The Ra Material: An Ancient Astronaut Speaks (Law of One),* 1984, Whitford Press

Schucman, Helen, *A Course In Miracles*, 1985, Foundation for Peace

Sitchin, Zecharia, *The 12ᵗʰ Planet (Book 1): The First Book of the Earth*, 1991, Bear & Company

Printed in the United States
By Bookmasters